IT'S NOT ABOUT TIME MANAGEMENT
IT'S ABOUT PRIORITY MANAGEMENT

TINA BLACK

BE A PLANNER

23 22 21 20 19 18   8 7 6 5 4 3 2 1

BE A PLANNER– It's not about time management, it's about priority management
©2018 Tina Black

emerge
publishing
TULSA, OKLAHOMA

Published by:
Emerge Publishing, LLC
9521B Riverside Parkway, Suite 243
Tulsa, Oklahoma 74137
Phone: 888.407.4447
www.EmergePublishing.com

ISBN: 978-0-9907694-0-8 Paperback

BISAC Category:
SEL035000   SELF-HELP / Self-Management / Time Management
SEL045000   SELF-HELP / Journaling
SEL027000   SELF-HELP / Personal Growth / Success

Author Contact:
Tina Black
2950 Lapeer Road
Port Huron, MI 48060
Tel: 810.987.8118
Email: tina@tinablack.net
Web: www.tinablack.net

ATTENTION: ORGANIZATIONS and CORPORATIONS
Bulk quantity discounts for reselling, gifts, or fundraising are available.
For more information, please contact Tina@tinablack.net.

20% of the proceeds from this book will go to the non-profit **Andrew Gomez Dream Foundation**, which provides educational support to cosmetology students and graduates and partners annually with other select charities to jointly raise funds.

Printed in the United States of America.

BE
BE A PLANNER

TABLE OF CONTENTS

INTRODUCTION

Welcome to BE A PLANNER!

I'll never forget the moment I forgot a very important meeting. I knew at the time that I had lost the trust of my mentor, and the words of my husband rang true for me that day. For years, he had told me to put all my tasks and meetings in my Google calendar, but I'd take offense every time he said it. I'd respond with, "No, I'd never forget an important meeting." Pointing to my head, I'd add, "It's all up here. I don't need to write it down." Famous last words . . .

The day I forgot that meeting, I immediately became a Google calendar wizard. But then, years later, while talking to my business partner, Winn Claybaugh, I looked over and saw him writing notes in a journal-type calendar. "What is that?" I asked.

"This is my calendar," he said. "I also print out important emails that I need to answer, and I keep important notes with me, so I don't forget things."

Now you need to understand: this man doesn't forget anything, from birthdays to responding to email to meetings. He's my role model for planning. I've never seen anything like it. So that day, I bought a planner and started experimenting with practically every planner in the universe. (Well, not really, but you get the point. Let me put it this way: I might have been a millionaire if I hadn't purchased all those planners! I'm addicted to planners and journals.)

Over the years, I developed my own journal pages and planning tools and made copies to put into planners I purchased—but I didn't give up my Google calendar. Instead of using one or the other, I found the perfect combination!

Now I use the Google calendar for what I like to call my "big rocks" (essential meetings, anniversaries, birthdays, etc.), and I also love my paper planner. First, there's not enough space to write and view everything easily on the Google calendar, especially on my phone, but seeing the whole month's calendar at a glance makes me feel like, "Okay, I've got this!" There's also something magical about putting pen to paper: it involves both the left brain (logical side) and right brain (creative side) and solidifies the information so it's even more memorable. When I only used my Google calendar, I still sometimes missed things, but now with my *BE A PLANNER* system, I don't miss a thing.

One day out of the blue, a fellow John Maxwell coach who had just read my first book, BE AMAZING, said, "Hey, you should design a planner. They're really hot right now." His belief in me birthed this planner! This book is a collection of all the yearly, monthly, weekly, and daily worksheets I've put together from the many different planners that inspired me over the years. Use them all or just a few, but the most important thing is to find what works for you and do it.

I hope you enjoy it. As the saying goes, if you fail to plan, then plan to fail.

And by the way, I hope you'll also join one of my online leadership mastermind groups to get even more inspiration. You'll find them at *www.tinablack.net*

Happy planning!

HOW TO USE THE PLANNERS AND WORKSHEETS

When I showed this planner to one of my team members, she said, *"This is everything I ever wanted in a planner!"* I think you'll agree.

I've been using these worksheets and sharing them with my coaching clients for years, and now you have them all in one book. Being a planner will make your life a lot easier and give you the focus you need to reach your life goals—and more important, to live out your God-given game plan. Just remember when you fill these out: It's not about time management, it's about priority management.

Throughout the planner, you'll notice colored tabs that describe when to use each worksheet: daily, weekly, monthly, quarterly, yearly. If you discipline yourself to use them all and trust the process, you'll have your best year ever!

Before you dive in, I'd like to share a few tips on how I use the planners and worksheets:

- I made all of the planners and worksheets customizable—you write in the month and the date—so you can start using this system at any time of the year.

- **Month-at-a-Glance Monthly Planners:** I use the monthly planners to capture my "big rocks" – my high priorities like birthdays, anniversaries, standing meetings, events, vacations, and anything else on my Google calendar. To make sure I don't neglect my top priorities, I put them in first and then fit the smaller rocks around them, not the other way around.

7

- **Week-at-a-Glance Daily Planners:** I use the daily planners to plan my day and my week. I start by checking my Google calendar and monthly planner to make sure I schedule everything else around the "big rocks." Then I fill in the remaining appointments, meetings, tasks, errands, and anything else I want to accomplish. Since weekends are usually lighter days, I combined Saturday and Sunday into a single column and made the hours customizable. I use the boxes at the bottom of the page to keep track of my progress in my personal development, areas I need to inspect in my companies, aspects of my job description (or roles) that I need to focus on that day, and how I create magic for my family, team, customers, etc.

- **Worksheets:** The second part of the book contains my favorite worksheets. You'll find instructions for each form at the beginning of each section.

P.S. If you'd like extra worksheet forms, you can download them from *www.tinablack.net*. Use the code **BE** to gain access.

BE A PLANNER
MONTHLY PLANNER

MONTH _____ YEAR _____

SUNDAY	MONDAY	TUESDAY	WEDNESDAY	THURSDAY	FRIDAY	SATURDAY

MONTH _____ YEAR _____

SUNDAY	MONDAY	TUESDAY	WEDNESDAY	THURSDAY	FRIDAY	SATURDAY

MONTH _____ YEAR _____

	SUNDAY	MONDAY	TUESDAY	WEDNESDAY	THURSDAY	FRIDAY	SATURDAY
MONTHLY PLANNER							

MONTH _____ YEAR _____

SUNDAY	MONDAY	TUESDAY	WEDNESDAY	THURSDAY	FRIDAY	SATURDAY

MONTH _____ YEAR _____

SUNDAY	MONDAY	TUESDAY	WEDNESDAY	THURSDAY	FRIDAY	SATURDAY

14

MONTH _____ YEAR _____

SUNDAY	MONDAY	TUESDAY	WEDNESDAY	THURSDAY	FRIDAY	SATURDAY

MONTH _____ YEAR _____

SUNDAY	MONDAY	TUESDAY	WEDNESDAY	THURSDAY	FRIDAY	SATURDAY

MONTH _____ YEAR _____

SUNDAY	MONDAY	TUESDAY	WEDNESDAY	THURSDAY	FRIDAY	SATURDAY

MONTH _____ YEAR _____

SUNDAY	MONDAY	TUESDAY	WEDNESDAY	THURSDAY	FRIDAY	SATURDAY

MONTH _____ YEAR _____

SUNDAY	MONDAY	TUESDAY	WEDNESDAY	THURSDAY	FRIDAY	SATURDAY

BE
BE A PLANNER

BE A PLANNER
DAILY PLANNER

Date _____

Date _____

Date _____

MONDAY	TUESDAY	WEDNESDAY
8:00 am	8:00 am	8:00 am
8:15 am	8:15 am	8:15 am
8:30 am	8:30 am	8:30 am
8:45 am	8:45 am	8:45 am
9:00 am	9:00 am	9:00 am
9:15 am	9:15 am	9:15 am
9:30 am	9:30 am	9:30 am
9:45 am	9:45 am	9:45 am
10:00 am	10:00 am	10:00 am
10:15 am	10:15 am	10:15 am
10:30 am	10:30 am	10.30 am
10:45 am	10:45 am	10:45 am
11:00 am	11:00 am	11:00 am
11:15 am	11:15 am	11:15 am
11:30 am	11:30 am	11:30 am
11:45 am	11:45 am	11:45 am
12:00 pm	12:00 pm	12:00 pm
12:15 pm	12:15 pm	12:15 pm
12:30 pm	12:30 pm	12:30 pm
12:45 pm	12:45 pm	12:45 pm
1:00 pm	1:00 pm	1:00 pm
1:15 pm	1:15 pm	1:15 pm
1:30 pm	1:30 pm	1:30 pm
1:45 pm	1:45 pm	1:45 pm
2:00 pm	2:00 pm	2:00 pm
2:15 pm	2:15 pm	2:15 pm
2:30 pm	2:30 pm	2:30 pm
2:45 pm	2:45 pm	2:45 pm
3:00 pm	3:00 pm	3:00 pm
3:15 pm	3:15 pm	3:15 pm
3:30 pm	3:30 pm	3:30 pm
3:45 pm	3:45 pm	3:45 pm
4:00 pm	4:00 pm	4:00 pm
4:15 pm	4:15 pm	4:15 pm
4:30 pm	4:30 pm	4:30 pm
4:45 pm	4:45 pm	4:45 pm
5:00 pm	5:00 pm	5:00 pm
5:15 pm	5:15 pm	5:15 pm
5:30 pm	5:30 pm	5:30 pm
5:45 pm	5:45 pm	5:45 pm
6:00 pm	6:00 pm	6:00 pm

TIME MANAGEMENT

PERSONAL DEVELOPMENT	INSPECT	JOB DESCRIPTION	CREATE MAGIC!

Date _____   Date _____   Date _____

THURSDAY	FRIDAY	SATURDAY
8:00 am	8:00 am	
8:15 am	8:15 am	
8:30 am	8:30 am	
8:45 am	8:45 am	
9:00 am	9:00 am	
9:15 am	9:15 am	
9:30 am	9:30 am	
9:45 am	9:45 am	
10:00 am	10:00 am	
10:15 am	10:15 am	
10:30 am	10:30 am	
10:45 am	10:45 am	
11:00 am	11:00 am	
11:15 am	11:15 am	
11:30 am	11:30 am	
11:45 am	11:45 am	
12:00 pm	12:00 pm	
12:15 pm	12:15 pm	
12:30 pm	12:30 pm	
12:45 pm	12:45 pm	
1:00 pm	1:00 pm	

		SUNDAY
1:15 pm	1:15 pm	
1:30 pm	1:30 pm	
1:45 pm	1:45 pm	
2:00 pm	2:00 pm	
2:15 pm	2:15 pm	
2:30 pm	2:30 pm	
2:45 pm	2:45 pm	
3:00 pm	3:00 pm	
3:15 pm	3:15 pm	
3:30 pm	3:30 pm	
3:45 pm	3:45 pm	
4:00 pm	4:00 pm	
4:15 pm	4:15 pm	
4:30 pm	4:30 pm	
4:45 pm	4:45 pm	
5:00 pm	5:00 pm	
5:15 pm	5:15 pm	
5:30 pm	5:30 pm	
5:45 pm	5:45 pm	
6:00 pm	6:00 pm	

TIME MANAGEMENT

PERSONAL DEVELOPMENT	INSPECT	JOB DESCRIPTION	CREATE MAGIC!

Date _____

MONDAY

8:00 am	
8:15 am	
8:30 am	
8:45 am	
9:00 am	
9:15 am	
9:30 am	
9:45 am	
10:00 am	
10:15 am	
10:30 am	
10:45 am	
11:00 am	
11:15 am	
11:30 am	
11:45 am	
12:00 pm	
12:15 pm	
12:30 pm	
12:45 pm	
1:00 pm	
1:15 pm	
1:30 pm	
1:45 pm	
2:00 pm	
2:15 pm	
2:30 pm	
2:45 pm	
3:00 pm	
3:15 pm	
3:30 pm	
3:45 pm	
4:00 pm	
4:15 pm	
4:30 pm	
4:45 pm	
5:00 pm	
5:15 pm	
5:30 pm	
5:45 pm	
6:00 pm	

Date _____

TUESDAY

8:00 am	
8:15 am	
8:30 am	
8:45 am	
9:00 am	
9:15 am	
9:30 am	
9:45 am	
10:00 am	
10:15 am	
10:30 am	
10:45 am	
11:00 am	
11:15 am	
11:30 am	
11:45 am	
12:00 pm	
12:15 pm	
12:30 pm	
12:45 pm	
1:00 pm	
1:15 pm	
1:30 pm	
1:45 pm	
2:00 pm	
2:15 pm	
2:30 pm	
2:45 pm	
3:00 pm	
3:15 pm	
3:30 pm	
3:45 pm	
4:00 pm	
4:15 pm	
4:30 pm	
4:45 pm	
5:00 pm	
5:15 pm	
5:30 pm	
5:45 pm	
6:00 pm	

Date _____

WEDNESDAY

8:00 am	
8:15 am	
8:30 am	
8:45 am	
9:00 am	
9:15 am	
9:30 am	
9:45 am	
10:00 am	
10:15 am	
10:30 am	
10:45 am	
11:00 am	
11:15 am	
11:30 am	
11:45 am	
12:00 pm	
12:15 pm	
12:30 pm	
12:45 pm	
1:00 pm	
1:15 pm	
1:30 pm	
1:45 pm	
2:00 pm	
2:15 pm	
2:30 pm	
2:45 pm	
3:00 pm	
3:15 pm	
3:30 pm	
3:45 pm	
4:00 pm	
4:15 pm	
4:30 pm	
4:45 pm	
5:00 pm	
5:15 pm	
5:30 pm	
5:45 pm	
6:00 pm	

TIME MANAGEMENT

PERSONAL DEVELOPMENT	INSPECT	JOB DESCRIPTION	CREATE MAGIC!

Date _____

THURSDAY

8:00 am	
8:15 am	
8:30 am	
8:45 am	
9:00 am	
9:15 am	
9:30 am	
9:45 am	
10:00 am	
10:15 am	
10:30 am	
10:45 am	
11:00 am	
11:15 am	
11:30 am	
11:45 am	
12:00 pm	
12:15 pm	
12:30 pm	
12:45 pm	
1:00 pm	
1:15 pm	
1:30 pm	
1:45 pm	
2:00 pm	
2:15 pm	
2:30 pm	
2:45 pm	
3:00 pm	
3:15 pm	
3:30 pm	
3:45 pm	
4:00 pm	
4:15 pm	
4:30 pm	
4:45 pm	
5:00 pm	
5:15 pm	
5:30 pm	
5:45 pm	
6:00 pm	

Date _____

FRIDAY

8:00 am	
8:15 am	
8:30 am	
8:45 am	
9:00 am	
9:15 am	
9:30 am	
9:45 am	
10:00 am	
10:15 am	
10:30 am	
10:45 am	
11:00 am	
11:15 am	
11:30 am	
11:45 am	
12:00 pm	
12:15 pm	
12:30 pm	
12:45 pm	
1:00 pm	
1:15 pm	
1:30 pm	
1:45 pm	
2:00 pm	
2:15 pm	
2:30 pm	
2:45 pm	
3:00 pm	
3:15 pm	
3:30 pm	
3:45 pm	
4:00 pm	
4:15 pm	
4:30 pm	
4:45 pm	
5:00 pm	
5:15 pm	
5:30 pm	
5:45 pm	
6:00 pm	

Date _____

SATURDAY

SUNDAY

TIME MANAGEMENT

PERSONAL DEVELOPMENT	INSPECT	JOB DESCRIPTION	CREATE MAGIC!

27

Date _____ Date _____ Date _____

MONDAY	TUESDAY	WEDNESDAY
8:00 am	8:00 am	8:00 am
8:15 am	8:15 am	8:15 am
8:30 am	8:30 am	8:30 am
8:45 am	8:45 am	8:45 am
9:00 am	9:00 am	9:00 am
9:15 am	9:15 am	9:15 am
9:30 am	9:30 am	9:30 am
9:45 am	9:45 am	9:45 am
10:00 am	10:00 am	10:00 am
10:15 am	10:15 am	10:15 am
10:30 am	10:30 am	10:30 am
10:45 am	10:45 am	10:45 am
11:00 am	11:00 am	11:00 am
11:15 am	11:15 am	11:15 am
11:30 am	11:30 am	11:30 am
11:45 am	11:45 am	11:45 am
12:00 pm	12:00 pm	12:00 pm
12:15 pm	12:15 pm	12:15 pm
12:30 pm	12:30 pm	12:30 pm
12:45 pm	12:45 pm	12:45 pm
1:00 pm	1:00 pm	1:00 pm
1:15 pm	1:15 pm	1:15 pm
1:30 pm	1:30 pm	1:30 pm
1:45 pm	1:45 pm	1:45 pm
2:00 pm	2:00 pm	2:00 pm
2:15 pm	2:15 pm	2:15 pm
2:30 pm	2:30 pm	2:30 pm
2:45 pm	2:45 pm	2:45 pm
3:00 pm	3:00 pm	3:00 pm
3:15 pm	3:15 pm	3:15 pm
3:30 pm	3:30 pm	3:30 pm
3:45 pm	3:45 pm	3:45 pm
4:00 pm	4:00 pm	4:00 pm
4:15 pm	4:15 pm	4:15 pm
4:30 pm	4:30 pm	4:30 pm
4:45 pm	4:45 pm	4:45 pm
5:00 pm	5:00 pm	5:00 pm
5:15 pm	5:15 pm	5:15 pm
5:30 pm	5:30 pm	5:30 pm
5:45 pm	5:45 pm	5:45 pm
6:00 pm	6:00 pm	6:00 pm

TIME MANAGEMENT

PERSONAL DEVELOPMENT	INSPECT	JOB DESCRIPTION	CREATE MAGIC!

Date _____   Date _____   Date _____

THURSDAY		FRIDAY		SATURDAY	
8:00 am		8:00 am			
8:15 am		8:15 am			
8:30 am		8:30 am			
8:45 am		8:45 am			
9:00 am		9:00 am			
9:15 am		9:15 am			
9:30 am		9:30 am			
9:45 am		9:45 am			
10:00 am		10:00 am			
10:15 am		10:15 am			
10:30 am		10:30 am			
10:45 am		10:45 am			
11:00 am		11:00 am			
11:15 am		11:15 am			
11:30 am		11:30 am			
11:45 am		11:45 am			
12:00 pm		12:00 pm			
12:15 pm		12:15 pm			
12:30 pm		12:30 pm			
12:45 pm		12:45 pm			
1:00 pm		1:00 pm			

SUNDAY

THURSDAY	FRIDAY
1:15 pm	1:15 pm
1:30 pm	1:30 pm
1:45 pm	1:45 pm
2:00 pm	2:00 pm
2:15 pm	2:15 pm
2:30 pm	2:30 pm
2:45 pm	2:45 pm
3:00 pm	3:00 pm
3:15 pm	3:15 pm
3:30 pm	3:30 pm
3:45 pm	3:45 pm
4:00 pm	4:00 pm
4:15 pm	4:15 pm
4:30 pm	4:30 pm
4:45 pm	4:45 pm
5:00 pm	5:00 pm
5:15 pm	5:15 pm
5:30 pm	5:30 pm
5:45 pm	5:45 pm
6:00 pm	6:00 pm

TIME MANAGEMENT

PERSONAL DEVELOPMENT	INSPECT	JOB DESCRIPTION	CREATE MAGIC!

Date _____

MONDAY

8:00 am	
8:15 am	
8:30 am	
8:45 am	
9:00 am	
9:15 am	
9:30 am	
9:45 am	
10:00 am	
10:15 am	
10:30 am	
10:45 am	
11:00 am	
11:15 am	
11:30 am	
11:45 am	
12:00 pm	
12:15 pm	
12:30 pm	
12:45 pm	
1:00 pm	
1:15 pm	
1:30 pm	
1:45 pm	
2:00 pm	
2:15 pm	
2:30 pm	
2:45 pm	
3:00 pm	
3:15 pm	
3:30 pm	
3:45 pm	
4:00 pm	
4:15 pm	
4:30 pm	
4:45 pm	
5:00 pm	
5:15 pm	
5:30 pm	
5:45 pm	
6:00 pm	

Date _____

TUESDAY

8:00 am	
8:15 am	
8:30 am	
8:45 am	
9:00 am	
9:15 am	
9:30 am	
9:45 am	
10:00 am	
10:15 am	
10:30 am	
10:45 am	
11:00 am	
11:15 am	
11:30 am	
11:45 am	
12:00 pm	
12:15 pm	
12:30 pm	
12:45 pm	
1:00 pm	
1:15 pm	
1:30 pm	
1:45 pm	
2:00 pm	
2:15 pm	
2:30 pm	
2:45 pm	
3:00 pm	
3:15 pm	
3:30 pm	
3:45 pm	
4:00 pm	
4:15 pm	
4:30 pm	
4:45 pm	
5:00 pm	
5:15 pm	
5:30 pm	
5:45 pm	
6:00 pm	

Date _____

WEDNESDAY

8:00 am	
8:15 am	
8:30 am	
8:45 am	
9:00 am	
9:15 am	
9:30 am	
9:45 am	
10:00 am	
10:15 am	
10:30 am	
10:45 am	
11:00 am	
11:15 am	
11:30 am	
11:45 am	
12:00 pm	
12:15 pm	
12:30 pm	
12:45 pm	
1:00 pm	
1:15 pm	
1:30 pm	
1:45 pm	
2:00 pm	
2:15 pm	
2:30 pm	
2:45 pm	
3:00 pm	
3:15 pm	
3:30 pm	
3:45 pm	
4:00 pm	
4:15 pm	
4:30 pm	
4:45 pm	
5:00 pm	
5:15 pm	
5:30 pm	
5:45 pm	
6:00 pm	

TIME MANAGEMENT

PERSONAL DEVELOPMENT	INSPECT	JOB DESCRIPTION	CREATE MAGIC!

Date _____   Date _____   Date _____

THURSDAY		FRIDAY		SATURDAY
8:00 am		8:00 am		
8:15 am		8:15 am		
8:30 am		8:30 am		
8:45 am		8:45 am		
9:00 am		9:00 am		
9:15 am		9:15 am		
9:30 am		9:30 am		
9:45 am		9:45 am		
10:00 am		10:00 am		
10:15 am		10:15 am		
10:30 am		10:30 am		
10:45 am		10:45 am		
11:00 am		11:00 am		
11:15 am		11:15 am		
11:30 am		11:30 am		
11:45 am		11:45 am		
12:00 pm		12:00 pm		
12:15 pm		12:15 pm		
12:30 pm		12:30 pm		
12:45 pm		12:45 pm		

				SUNDAY
1:00 pm		1:00 pm		
1:15 pm		1:15 pm		
1:30 pm		1:30 pm		
1:45 pm		1:45 pm		
2:00 pm		2:00 pm		
2:15 pm		2:15 pm		
2:30 pm		2:30 pm		
2:45 pm		2:45 pm		
3:00 pm		3:00 pm		
3:15 pm		3:15 pm		
3:30 pm		3:30 pm		
3:45 pm		3:45 pm		
4:00 pm		4:00 pm		
4:15 pm		4:15 pm		
4:30 pm		4:30 pm		
4:45 pm		4:45 pm		
5:00 pm		5:00 pm		
5:15 pm		5:15 pm		
5:30 pm		5:30 pm		
5:45 pm		5:45 pm		
6:00 pm		6:00 pm		

TIME MANAGEMENT

PERSONAL DEVELOPMENT	INSPECT	JOB DESCRIPTION	CREATE MAGIC!

33

Date _____ | Date _____ | Date _____

MONDAY	TUESDAY	WEDNESDAY
8:00 am	8:00 am	8:00 am
8:15 am	8:15 am	8:15 am
8:30 am	8:30 am	8:30 am
8:45 am	8:45 am	8:45 am
9:00 am	9:00 am	9:00 am
9:15 am	9:15 am	9:15 am
9:30 am	9:30 am	9:30 am
9:45 am	9:45 am	9:45 am
10:00 am	10:00 am	10:00 am
10:15 am	10:15 am	10:15 am
10:30 am	10:30 am	10:30 am
10:45 am	10:45 am	10:45 am
11:00 am	11:00 am	11:00 am
11:15 am	11:15 am	11:15 am
11:30 am	11:30 am	11:30 am
11:45 am	11:45 am	11:45 am
12:00 pm	12:00 pm	12:00 pm
12:15 pm	12:15 pm	12:15 pm
12:30 pm	12:30 pm	12:30 pm
12:45 pm	12:45 pm	12:45 pm
1:00 pm	1:00 pm	1:00 pm
1:15 pm	1:15 pm	1:15 pm
1:30 pm	1:30 pm	1:30 pm
1:45 pm	1:45 pm	1:45 pm
2:00 pm	2:00 pm	2:00 pm
2:15 pm	2:15 pm	2:15 pm
2:30 pm	2:30 pm	2:30 pm
2:45 pm	2:45 pm	2:45 pm
3:00 pm	3:00 pm	3:00 pm
3:15 pm	3:15 pm	3:15 pm
3:30 pm	3:30 pm	3:30 pm
3:45 pm	3:45 pm	3:45 pm
4:00 pm	4:00 pm	4:00 pm
4:15 pm	4:15 pm	4:15 pm
4:30 pm	4:30 pm	4:30 pm
4:45 pm	4:45 pm	4:45 pm
5:00 pm	5:00 pm	5:00 pm
5:15 pm	5:15 pm	5:15 pm
5:30 pm	5:30 pm	5:30 pm
5:45 pm	5:45 pm	5:45 pm
6:00 pm	6:00 pm	6:00 pm

TIME MANAGEMENT

PERSONAL DEVELOPMENT	INSPECT	JOB DESCRIPTION	CREATE MAGIC!

Date _____ Date _____ Date _____

THURSDAY	FRIDAY	SATURDAY

THURSDAY	FRIDAY	SATURDAY
8:00 am	8:00 am	
8:15 am	8:15 am	
8:30 am	8:30 am	
8:45 am	8:45 am	
9:00 am	9:00 am	
9:15 am	9:15 am	
9:30 am	9:30 am	
9:45 am	9:45 am	
10:00 am	10:00 am	
10:15 am	10:15 am	
10:30 am	10:30 am	
10:45 am	10:45 am	
11:00 am	11:00 am	
11:15 am	11:15 am	
11:30 am	11:30 am	
11:45 am	11:45 am	
12:00 pm	12:00 pm	
12:15 pm	12:15 pm	
12:30 pm	12:30 pm	
12:45 pm	12:45 pm	
1:00 pm	1:00 pm	

		SUNDAY
1:15 pm	1:15 pm	
1:30 pm	1:30 pm	
1:45 pm	1:45 pm	
2:00 pm	2:00 pm	
2:15 pm	2:15 pm	
2:30 pm	2:30 pm	
2:45 pm	2:45 pm	
3:00 pm	3:00 pm	
3:15 pm	3:15 pm	
3:30 pm	3:30 pm	
3:45 pm	3:45 pm	
4:00 pm	4:00 pm	
4:15 pm	4:15 pm	
4:30 pm	4:30 pm	
4:45 pm	4:45 pm	
5:00 pm	5:00 pm	
5:15 pm	5:15 pm	
5:30 pm	5:30 pm	
5:45 pm	5:45 pm	
6:00 pm	6:00 pm	

TIME MANAGEMENT

PERSONAL DEVELOPMENT	INSPECT	JOB DESCRIPTION	CREATE MAGIC!

DAILY PLANNER

MONDAY	TUESDAY	WEDNESDAY
8:00 am	8:00 am	8:00 am
8:15 am	8:15 am	8:15 am
8:30 am	8:30 am	8:30 am
8:45 am	8:45 am	8:45 am
9:00 am	9:00 am	9:00 am
9:15 am	9:15 am	9:15 am
9:30 am	9:30 am	9:30 am
9:45 am	9:45 am	9:45 am
10:00 am	10:00 am	10:00 am
10:15 am	10:15 am	10:15 am
10:30 am	10:30 am	10:30 am
10:45 am	10:45 am	10:45 am
11:00 am	11:00 am	11:00 am
11:15 am	11:15 am	11:15 am
11:30 am	11:30 am	11:30 am
11:45 am	11:45 am	11:45 am
12:00 pm	12:00 pm	12:00 pm
12:15 pm	12:15 pm	12:15 pm
12:30 pm	12:30 pm	12:30 pm
12:45 pm	12:45 pm	12:45 pm
1:00 pm	1:00 pm	1:00 pm
1:15 pm	1:15 pm	1:15 pm
1:30 pm	1:30 pm	1:30 pm
1:45 pm	1:45 pm	1:45 pm
2:00 pm	2:00 pm	2:00 pm
2:15 pm	2:15 pm	2:15 pm
2:30 pm	2:30 pm	2:30 pm
2:45 pm	2:45 pm	2:45 pm
3:00 pm	3:00 pm	3:00 pm
3:15 pm	3:15 pm	3:15 pm
3:30 pm	3:30 pm	3:30 pm
3:45 pm	3:45 pm	3:45 pm
4:00 pm	4:00 pm	4:00 pm
4:15 pm	4:15 pm	4:15 pm
4:30 pm	4:30 pm	4:30 pm
4:45 pm	4:45 pm	4:45 pm
5:00 pm	5:00 pm	5:00 pm
5:15 pm	5:15 pm	5:15 pm
5:30 pm	5:30 pm	5:30 pm
5:45 pm	5:45 pm	5:45 pm
6:00 pm	6:00 pm	6:00 pm

TIME MANAGEMENT

PERSONAL DEVELOPMENT	INSPECT	JOB DESCRIPTION	CREATE MAGIC!

Date _____ Date _____ Date _____

THURSDAY		FRIDAY		SATURDAY
8:00 am		8:00 am		
8:15 am		8:15 am		
8:30 am		8:30 am		
8:45 am		8:45 am		
9:00 am		9:00 am		
9:15 am		9:15 am		
9:30 am		9:30 am		
9:45 am		9:45 am		
10:00 am		10:00 am		
10:15 am		10:15 am		
10:30 am		10:30 am		
10:45 am		10:45 am		
11:00 am		11:00 am		
11:15 am		11:15 am		
11:30 am		11:30 am		
11:45 am		11:45 am		
12:00 pm		12:00 pm		
12:15 pm		12:15 pm		
12:30 pm		12:30 pm		
12:45 pm		12:45 pm		

THURSDAY	FRIDAY	SUNDAY
1:00 pm	1:00 pm	
1:15 pm	1:15 pm	
1:30 pm	1:30 pm	
1:45 pm	1:45 pm	
2:00 pm	2:00 pm	
2:15 pm	2:15 pm	
2:30 pm	2:30 pm	
2:45 pm	2:45 pm	
3:00 pm	3:00 pm	
3:15 pm	3:15 pm	
3:30 pm	3:30 pm	
3:45 pm	3:45 pm	
4:00 pm	4:00 pm	
4:15 pm	4:15 pm	
4:30 pm	4:30 pm	
4:45 pm	4:45 pm	
5:00 pm	5:00 pm	
5:15 pm	5:15 pm	
5:30 pm	5:30 pm	
5:45 pm	5:45 pm	
6:00 pm	6:00 pm	

DAILY PLANNER

TIME MANAGEMENT			
PERSONAL DEVELOPMENT	INSPECT	JOB DESCRIPTION	CREATE MAGIC!

37

Date _____ Date _____ Date _____

MONDAY	TUESDAY	WEDNESDAY
8:00 am	8:00 am	8:00 am
8:15 am	8:15 am	8:15 am
8:30 am	8:30 am	8:30 am
8:45 am	8:45 am	8:45 am
9:00 am	9:00 am	9:00 am
9:15 am	9:15 am	9:15 am
9:30 am	9:30 am	9:30 am
9:45 am	9:45 am	9:45 am
10:00 am	10:00 am	10:00 am
10:15 am	10:15 am	10:15 am
10:30 am	10:30 am	10:30 am
10:45 am	10:45 am	10:45 am
11:00 am	11:00 am	11:00 am
11:15 am	11:15 am	11:15 am
11:30 am	11:30 am	11:30 am
11:45 am	11:45 am	11:45 am
12:00 pm	12:00 pm	12:00 pm
12:15 pm	12:15 pm	12:15 pm
12:30 pm	12:30 pm	12:30 pm
12:45 pm	12:45 pm	12:45 pm
1:00 pm	1:00 pm	1:00 pm
1:15 pm	1:15 pm	1:15 pm
1:30 pm	1:30 pm	1:30 pm
1:45 pm	1:45 pm	1:45 pm
2:00 pm	2:00 pm	2:00 pm
2:15 pm	2:15 pm	2:15 pm
2:30 pm	2:30 pm	2:30 pm
2:45 pm	2:45 pm	2:45 pm
3:00 pm	3:00 pm	3:00 pm
3:15 pm	3:15 pm	3:15 pm
3:30 pm	3:30 pm	3:30 pm
3:45 pm	3:45 pm	3:45 pm
4:00 pm	4:00 pm	4:00 pm
4:15 pm	4:15 pm	4:15 pm
4:30 pm	4:30 pm	4:30 pm
4:45 pm	4:45 pm	4:45 pm
5:00 pm	5:00 pm	5:00 pm
5:15 pm	5:15 pm	5:15 pm
5:30 pm	5:30 pm	5:30 pm
5:45 pm	5:45 pm	5:45 pm
6:00 pm	6:00 pm	6:00 pm

TIME MANAGEMENT

PERSONAL DEVELOPMENT	INSPECT	JOB DESCRIPTION	CREATE MAGIC!

Date _____

THURSDAY

8:00 am	
8:15 am	
8:30 am	
8:45 am	
9:00 am	
9:15 am	
9:30 am	
9:45 am	
10:00 am	
10:15 am	
10:30 am	
10:45 am	
11:00 am	
11:15 am	
11:30 am	
11:45 am	
12:00 pm	
12:15 pm	
12:30 pm	
12:45 pm	
1:00 pm	
1:15 pm	
1:30 pm	
1:45 pm	
2:00 pm	
2:15 pm	
2:30 pm	
2:45 pm	
3:00 pm	
3:15 pm	
3:30 pm	
3:45 pm	
4:00 pm	
4:15 pm	
4:30 pm	
4:45 pm	
5:00 pm	
5:15 pm	
5:30 pm	
5:45 pm	
6:00 pm	

Date _____

FRIDAY

8:00 am	
8:15 am	
8:30 am	
8:45 am	
9:00 am	
9:15 am	
9:30 am	
9:45 am	
10:00 am	
10:15 am	
10:30 am	
10:45 am	
11:00 am	
11:15 am	
11:30 am	
11:45 am	
12:00 pm	
12:15 pm	
12:30 pm	
12:45 pm	
1:00 pm	
1:15 pm	
1:30 pm	
1:45 pm	
2:00 pm	
2:15 pm	
2:30 pm	
2:45 pm	
3:00 pm	
3:15 pm	
3:30 pm	
3:45 pm	
4:00 pm	
4:15 pm	
4:30 pm	
4:45 pm	
5:00 pm	
5:15 pm	
5:30 pm	
5:45 pm	
6:00 pm	

Date _____

SATURDAY

SUNDAY

TIME MANAGEMENT

PERSONAL DEVELOPMENT	INSPECT	JOB DESCRIPTION	CREATE MAGIC!

Date _____   Date _____   Date _____

MONDAY	TUESDAY	WEDNESDAY
8:00 am	8:00 am	8:00 am
8:15 am	8:15 am	8:15 am
8:30 am	8:30 am	8:30 am
8:45 am	8:45 am	8:45 am
9:00 am	9:00 am	9:00 am
9:15 am	9:15 am	9:15 am
9:30 am	9:30 am	9:30 am
9:45 am	9:45 am	9:45 am
10:00 am	10:00 am	10:00 am
10:15 am	10:15 am	10:15 am
10:30 am	10:30 am	10:30 am
10:45 am	10:45 am	10:45 am
11:00 am	11:00 am	11:00 am
11:15 am	11:15 am	11:15 am
11:30 am	11:30 am	11:30 am
11:45 am	11:45 am	11:45 am
12:00 pm	12:00 pm	12:00 pm
12:15 pm	12:15 pm	12:15 pm
12:30 pm	12:30 pm	12:30 pm
12:45 pm	12:45 pm	12:45 pm
1:00 pm	1:00 pm	1:00 pm
1:15 pm	1:15 pm	1:15 pm
1:30 pm	1:30 pm	1:30 pm
1:45 pm	1:45 pm	1:45 pm
2:00 pm	2:00 pm	2:00 pm
2:15 pm	2:15 pm	2:15 pm
2:30 pm	2:30 pm	2:30 pm
2:45 pm	2:45 pm	2:45 pm
3:00 pm	3:00 pm	3:00 pm
3:15 pm	3:15 pm	3:15 pm
3:30 pm	3:30 pm	3:30 pm
3:45 pm	3:45 pm	3:45 pm
4:00 pm	4:00 pm	4:00 pm
4:15 pm	4:15 pm	4:15 pm
4:30 pm	4:30 pm	4:30 pm
4:45 pm	4:45 pm	4:45 pm
5:00 pm	5:00 pm	5:00 pm
5:15 pm	5:15 pm	5:15 pm
5:30 pm	5:30 pm	5:30 pm
5:45 pm	5:45 pm	5:45 pm
6:00 pm	6:00 pm	6:00 pm

TIME MANAGEMENT

PERSONAL DEVELOPMENT	INSPECT	JOB DESCRIPTION	CREATE MAGIC!

Date _____   Date _____   Date _____

THURSDAY		FRIDAY		SATURDAY
8:00 am		8:00 am		
8:15 am		8:15 am		
8:30 am		8:30 am		
8:45 am		8:45 am		
9:00 am		9:00 am		
9:15 am		9:15 am		
9:30 am		9:30 am		
9:45 am		9:45 am		
10:00 am		10:00 am		
10:15 am		10:15 am		
10:30 am		10:30 am		
10:45 am		10:45 am		
11:00 am		11:00 am		
11:15 am		11:15 am		
11:30 am		11:30 am		
11:45 am		11:45 am		
12:00 pm		12:00 pm		
12:15 pm		12:15 pm		
12:30 pm		12:30 pm		
12:45 pm		12:45 pm		
1:00 pm		1:00 pm		

				SUNDAY
1:15 pm		1:15 pm		
1:30 pm		1:30 pm		
1:45 pm		1:45 pm		
2:00 pm		2:00 pm		
2:15 pm		2:15 pm		
2:30 pm		2:30 pm		
2:45 pm		2:45 pm		
3:00 pm		3:00 pm		
3:15 pm		3:15 pm		
3:30 pm		3:30 pm		
3:45 pm		3:45 pm		
4:00 pm		4:00 pm		
4:15 pm		4:15 pm		
4:30 pm		4:30 pm		
4:45 pm		4:45 pm		
5:00 pm		5:00 pm		
5:15 pm		5:15 pm		
5:30 pm		5:30 pm		
5:45 pm		5:45 pm		
6:00 pm		6:00 pm		

TIME MANAGEMENT

PERSONAL DEVELOPMENT	INSPECT	JOB DESCRIPTION	CREATE MAGIC!

Date _____   Date _____   Date _____

MONDAY	TUESDAY	WEDNESDAY
8:00 am	8:00 am	8:00 am
8:15 am	8:15 am	8:15 am
8:30 am	8:30 am	8:30 am
8:45 am	8:45 am	8:45 am
9:00 am	9:00 am	9:00 am
9:15 am	9:15 am	9:15 am
9:30 am	9:30 am	9:30 am
9:45 am	9:45 am	9:45 am
10:00 am	10:00 am	10:00 am
10:15 am	10:15 am	10:15 am
10:30 am	10:30 am	10:30 am
10:45 am	10:45 am	10:45 am
11:00 am	11:00 am	11:00 am
11:15 am	11:15 am	11:15 am
11:30 am	11:30 am	11:30 am
11:45 am	11:45 am	11:45 am
12:00 pm	12:00 pm	12:00 pm
12:15 pm	12:15 pm	12:15 pm
12:30 pm	12:30 pm	12:30 pm
12:45 pm	12:45 pm	12:45 pm
1:00 pm	1:00 pm	1:00 pm
1:15 pm	1:15 pm	1:15 pm
1:30 pm	1:30 pm	1:30 pm
1:45 pm	1:45 pm	1:45 pm
2:00 pm	2:00 pm	2:00 pm
2:15 pm	2:15 pm	2:15 pm
2:30 pm	2:30 pm	2:30 pm
2:45 pm	2:45 pm	2:45 pm
3:00 pm	3:00 pm	3:00 pm
3:15 pm	3:15 pm	3:15 pm
3:30 pm	3:30 pm	3:30 pm
3:45 pm	3:45 pm	3:45 pm
4:00 pm	4:00 pm	4:00 pm
4:15 pm	4:15 pm	4:15 pm
4:30 pm	4:30 pm	4:30 pm
4:45 pm	4:45 pm	4:45 pm
5:00 pm	5:00 pm	5:00 pm
5:15 pm	5:15 pm	5:15 pm
5:30 pm	5:30 pm	5:30 pm
5:45 pm	5:45 pm	5:45 pm
6:00 pm	6:00 pm	6:00 pm

TIME MANAGEMENT

PERSONAL DEVELOPMENT	INSPECT	JOB DESCRIPTION	CREATE MAGIC!

Date _____ Date _____ Date _____

THURSDAY	FRIDAY	SATURDAY

THURSDAY	FRIDAY
8:00 am	8:00 am
8:15 am	8:15 am
8:30 am	8:30 am
8:45 am	8:45 am
9:00 am	9:00 am
9:15 am	9:15 am
9:30 am	9:30 am
9:45 am	9:45 am
10:00 am	10:00 am
10:15 am	10:15 am
10:30 am	10:30 am
10:45 am	10:45 am
11:00 am	11:00 am
11:15 am	11:15 am
11:30 am	11:30 am
11:45 am	11:45 am
12:00 pm	12:00 pm
12:15 pm	12:15 pm
12:30 pm	12:30 pm
12:45 pm	12:45 pm
1:00 pm	1:00 pm
1:15 pm	1:15 pm
1:30 pm	1:30 pm
1:45 pm	1:45 pm
2:00 pm	2:00 pm
2:15 pm	2:15 pm
2:30 pm	2:30 pm
2:45 pm	2:45 pm
3:00 pm	3:00 pm
3:15 pm	3:15 pm
3:30 pm	3:30 pm
3:45 pm	3:45 pm
4:00 pm	4:00 pm
4:15 pm	4:15 pm
4:30 pm	4:30 pm
4:45 pm	4:45 pm
5:00 pm	5:00 pm
5:15 pm	5:15 pm
5:30 pm	5:30 pm
5:45 pm	5:45 pm
6:00 pm	6:00 pm

SUNDAY

TIME MANAGEMENT

PERSONAL DEVELOPMENT	INSPECT	JOB DESCRIPTION	CREATE MAGIC!

43

Date _____   Date _____   Date _____

MONDAY	TUESDAY	WEDNESDAY
8:00 am	8:00 am	8:00 am
8:15 am	8:15 am	8:15 am
8:30 am	8:30 am	8:30 am
8:45 am	8:45 am	8:45 am
9:00 am	9:00 am	9:00 am
9:15 am	9:15 am	9:15 am
9:30 am	9:30 am	9:30 am
9:45 am	9:45 am	9:45 am
10:00 am	10:00 am	10:00 am
10:15 am	10:15 am	10:15 am
10:30 am	10:30 am	10:30 am
10:45 am	10:45 am	10:45 am
11:00 am	11:00 am	11:00 am
11:15 am	11:15 am	11:15 am
11:30 am	11:30 am	11:30 am
11:45 am	11:45 am	11:45 am
12:00 pm	12:00 pm	12:00 pm
12:15 pm	12:15 pm	12:15 pm
12:30 pm	12:30 pm	12:30 pm
12:45 pm	12:45 pm	12:45 pm
1:00 pm	1:00 pm	1:00 pm
1:15 pm	1:15 pm	1:15 pm
1:30 pm	1:30 pm	1:30 pm
1:45 pm	1:45 pm	1:45 pm
2:00 pm	2:00 pm	2:00 pm
2:15 pm	2:15 pm	2:15 pm
2:30 pm	2:30 pm	2:30 pm
2:45 pm	2:45 pm	2:45 pm
3:00 pm	3:00 pm	3:00 pm
3:15 pm	3:15 pm	3:15 pm
3:30 pm	3:30 pm	3:30 pm
3:45 pm	3:45 pm	3:45 pm
4:00 pm	4:00 pm	4:00 pm
4:15 pm	4:15 pm	4:15 pm
4:30 pm	4:30 pm	4:30 pm
4:45 pm	4:45 pm	4:45 pm
5:00 pm	5:00 pm	5:00 pm
5:15 pm	5:15 pm	5:15 pm
5:30 pm	5:30 pm	5:30 pm
5:45 pm	5:45 pm	5:45 pm
6:00 pm	6:00 pm	6:00 pm

TIME MANAGEMENT

PERSONAL DEVELOPMENT	INSPECT	JOB DESCRIPTION	CREATE MAGIC!

Date _____ Date _____ Date _____

THURSDAY	FRIDAY	SATURDAY
8:00 am	8:00 am	
8:15 am	8:15 am	
8:30 am	8:30 am	
8:45 am	8:45 am	
9:00 am	9:00 am	
9:15 am	9:15 am	
9:30 am	9:30 am	
9:45 am	9:45 am	
10:00 am	10:00 am	
10:15 am	10:15 am	
10:30 am	10:30 am	
10:45 am	10:45 am	
11:00 am	11:00 am	
11:15 am	11:15 am	
11:30 am	11:30 am	
11:45 am	11:45 am	
12:00 pm	12:00 pm	
12:15 pm	12:15 pm	
12:30 pm	12:30 pm	
12:45 pm	12:45 pm	

THURSDAY	FRIDAY	SUNDAY
1:00 pm	1:00 pm	
1:15 pm	1:15 pm	
1:30 pm	1:30 pm	
1:45 pm	1:45 pm	
2:00 pm	2:00 pm	
2:15 pm	2:15 pm	
2:30 pm	2:30 pm	
2:45 pm	2:45 pm	
3:00 pm	3:00 pm	
3:15 pm	3:15 pm	
3:30 pm	3:30 pm	
3:45 pm	3:45 pm	
4:00 pm	4:00 pm	
4:15 pm	4:15 pm	
4:30 pm	4:30 pm	
4:45 pm	4:45 pm	
5:00 pm	5:00 pm	
5:15 pm	5:15 pm	
5:30 pm	5:30 pm	
5:45 pm	5:45 pm	
6:00 pm	6:00 pm	

TIME MANAGEMENT

PERSONAL DEVELOPMENT	INSPECT	JOB DESCRIPTION	CREATE MAGIC!

Date _____

Date _____

Date _____

MONDAY	TUESDAY	WEDNESDAY
8:00 am	8:00 am	8:00 am
8:15 am	8:15 am	8:15 am
8:30 am	8:30 am	8:30 am
8:45 am	8:45 am	8:45 am
9:00 am	9:00 am	9:00 am
9:15 am	9:15 am	9:15 am
9:30 am	9:30 am	9:30 am
9:45 am	9:45 am	9:45 am
10:00 am	10:00 am	10:00 am
10:15 am	10:15 am	10:15 am
10:30 am	10:30 am	10:30 am
10:45 am	10:45 am	10:45 am
11:00 am	11:00 am	11:00 am
11:15 am	11:15 am	11:15 am
11:30 am	11:30 am	11:30 am
11:45 am	11:45 am	11:45 am
12:00 pm	12:00 pm	12:00 pm
12:15 pm	12:15 pm	12:15 pm
12:30 pm	12:30 pm	12:30 pm
12:45 pm	12:45 pm	12:45 pm
1:00 pm	1:00 pm	1:00 pm
1:15 pm	1:15 pm	1:15 pm
1:30 pm	1:30 pm	1:30 pm
1:45 pm	1:45 pm	1:45 pm
2:00 pm	2:00 pm	2:00 pm
2:15 pm	2:15 pm	2:15 pm
2:30 pm	2:30 pm	2:30 pm
2:45 pm	2:45 pm	2:45 pm
3:00 pm	3:00 pm	3:00 pm
3:15 pm	3:15 pm	3:15 pm
3:30 pm	3:30 pm	3:30 pm
3:45 pm	3:45 pm	3:45 pm
4:00 pm	4:00 pm	4:00 pm
4:15 pm	4:15 pm	4:15 pm
4:30 pm	4:30 pm	4:30 pm
4:45 pm	4:45 pm	4:45 pm
5:00 pm	5:00 pm	5:00 pm
5:15 pm	5:15 pm	5:15 pm
5:30 pm	5:30 pm	5:30 pm
5:45 pm	5:45 pm	5:45 pm
6:00 pm	6:00 pm	6:00 pm

TIME MANAGEMENT

PERSONAL DEVELOPMENT	INSPECT	JOB DESCRIPTION	CREATE MAGIC!

Date _____ Date _____ Date _____

THURSDAY	FRIDAY	SATURDAY
8:00 am	8:00 am	
8:15 am	8:15 am	
8:30 am	8:30 am	
8:45 am	8:45 am	
9:00 am	9:00 am	
9:15 am	9:15 am	
9:30 am	9:30 am	
9:45 am	9:45 am	
10:00 am	10:00 am	
10:15 am	10:15 am	
10:30 am	10:30 am	
10:45 am	10:45 am	
11:00 am	11:00 am	
11:15 am	11:15 am	
11:30 am	11:30 am	
11:45 am	11:45 am	
12:00 pm	12:00 pm	
12:15 pm	12:15 pm	
12:30 pm	12:30 pm	
12:45 pm	12:45 pm	
1:00 pm	1:00 pm	

SUNDAY

THURSDAY	FRIDAY	SUNDAY
1:15 pm	1:15 pm	
1:30 pm	1:30 pm	
1:45 pm	1:45 pm	
2:00 pm	2:00 pm	
2:15 pm	2:15 pm	
2:30 pm	2:30 pm	
2:45 pm	2:45 pm	
3:00 pm	3:00 pm	
3:15 pm	3:15 pm	
3:30 pm	3:30 pm	
3:45 pm	3:45 pm	
4:00 pm	4:00 pm	
4:15 pm	4:15 pm	
4:30 pm	4:30 pm	
4:45 pm	4:45 pm	
5:00 pm	5:00 pm	
5:15 pm	5:15 pm	
5:30 pm	5:30 pm	
5:45 pm	5:45 pm	
6:00 pm	6:00 pm	

TIME MANAGEMENT

PERSONAL DEVELOPMENT	INSPECT	JOB DESCRIPTION	CREATE MAGIC!

47

DAILY PLANNER

MONDAY	TUESDAY	WEDNESDAY
8:00 am	8:00 am	8:00 am
8:15 am	8:15 am	8:15 am
8:30 am	8:30 am	8:30 am
8:45 am	8:45 am	8:45 am
9:00 am	9:00 am	9:00 am
9:15 am	9:15 am	9:15 am
9:30 am	9:30 am	9:30 am
9:45 am	9:45 am	9:45 am
10:00 am	10:00 am	10:00 am
10:15 am	10:15 am	10:15 am
10:30 am	10:30 am	10:30 am
10:45 am	10:45 am	10:45 am
11:00 am	11:00 am	11:00 am
11:15 am	11:15 am	11:15 am
11:30 am	11:30 am	11:30 am
11:45 am	11:45 am	11:45 am
12:00 pm	12:00 pm	12:00 pm
12:15 pm	12:15 pm	12:15 pm
12:30 pm	12:30 pm	12:30 pm
12:45 pm	12:45 pm	12:45 pm
1:00 pm	1:00 pm	1:00 pm
1:15 pm	1:15 pm	1:15 pm
1:30 pm	1:30 pm	1:30 pm
1:45 pm	1:45 pm	1:45 pm
2:00 pm	2:00 pm	2:00 pm
2:15 pm	2:15 pm	2:15 pm
2:30 pm	2:30 pm	2:30 pm
2:45 pm	2:45 pm	2:45 pm
3:00 pm	3:00 pm	3:00 pm
3:15 pm	3:15 pm	3:15 pm
3:30 pm	3:30 pm	3:30 pm
3:45 pm	3:45 pm	3:45 pm
4:00 pm	4:00 pm	4:00 pm
4:15 pm	4:15 pm	4:15 pm
4:30 pm	4:30 pm	4:30 pm
4:45 pm	4:45 pm	4:45 pm
5:00 pm	5:00 pm	5:00 pm
5:15 pm	5:15 pm	5:15 pm
5:30 pm	5:30 pm	5:30 pm
5:45 pm	5:45 pm	5:45 pm
6:00 pm	6:00 pm	6:00 pm

TIME MANAGEMENT

PERSONAL DEVELOPMENT	INSPECT	JOB DESCRIPTION	CREATE MAGIC!

Date _____   Date _____   Date _____

THURSDAY		FRIDAY		SATURDAY
8:00 am		8:00 am		
8:15 am		8:15 am		
8:30 am		8:30 am		
8:45 am		8:45 am		
9:00 am		9:00 am		
9:15 am		9:15 am		
9:30 am		9:30 am		
9:45 am		9:45 am		
10:00 am		10:00 am		
10:15 am		10:15 am		
10:30 am		10:30 am		
10:45 am		10:45 am		
11:00 am		11:00 am		
11:15 am		11:15 am		
11:30 am		11:30 am		
11:45 am		11:45 am		
12:00 pm		12:00 pm		
12:15 pm		12:15 pm		
12:30 pm		12:30 pm		
12:45 pm		12:45 pm		
1:00 pm		1:00 pm		**SUNDAY**
1:15 pm		1:15 pm		
1:30 pm		1:30 pm		
1:45 pm		1:45 pm		
2:00 pm		2:00 pm		
2:15 pm		2:15 pm		
2:30 pm		2:30 pm		
2:45 pm		2:45 pm		
3:00 pm		3:00 pm		
3:15 pm		3:15 pm		
3:30 pm		3:30 pm		
3:45 pm		3:45 pm		
4:00 pm		4:00 pm		
4:15 pm		4:15 pm		
4:30 pm		4:30 pm		
4:45 pm		4:45 pm		
5:00 pm		5:00 pm		
5:15 pm		5:15 pm		
5:30 pm		5:30 pm		
5:45 pm		5:45 pm		
6:00 pm		6:00 pm		

TIME MANAGEMENT

PERSONAL DEVELOPMENT	INSPECT	JOB DESCRIPTION	CREATE MAGIC!

Date _____

MONDAY

8:00 am	
8:15 am	
8:30 am	
8:45 am	
9:00 am	
9:15 am	
9:30 am	
9:45 am	
10:00 am	
10:15 am	
10:30 am	
10:45 am	
11:00 am	
11:15 am	
11:30 am	
11:45 am	
12:00 pm	
12:15 pm	
12:30 pm	
12:45 pm	
1:00 pm	
1:15 pm	
1:30 pm	
1:45 pm	
2:00 pm	
2:15 pm	
2:30 pm	
2:45 pm	
3:00 pm	
3:15 pm	
3:30 pm	
3:45 pm	
4:00 pm	
4:15 pm	
4:30 pm	
4:45 pm	
5:00 pm	
5:15 pm	
5:30 pm	
5:45 pm	
6:00 pm	

Date _____

TUESDAY

8:00 am	
8:15 am	
8:30 am	
8:45 am	
9:00 am	
9:15 am	
9:30 am	
9:45 am	
10:00 am	
10:15 am	
10:30 am	
10:45 am	
11:00 am	
11:15 am	
11:30 am	
11:45 am	
12:00 pm	
12:15 pm	
12:30 pm	
12:45 pm	
1:00 pm	
1:15 pm	
1:30 pm	
1:45 pm	
2:00 pm	
2:15 pm	
2:30 pm	
2:45 pm	
3:00 pm	
3:15 pm	
3:30 pm	
3:45 pm	
4:00 pm	
4:15 pm	
4:30 pm	
4:45 pm	
5:00 pm	
5:15 pm	
5:30 pm	
5:45 pm	
6:00 pm	

Date _____

WEDNESDAY

8:00 am	
8:15 am	
8:30 am	
8:45 am	
9:00 am	
9:15 am	
9:30 am	
9:45 am	
10:00 am	
10:15 am	
10:30 am	
10:45 am	
11:00 am	
11:15 am	
11:30 am	
11:45 am	
12:00 pm	
12:15 pm	
12:30 pm	
12:45 pm	
1:00 pm	
1:15 pm	
1:30 pm	
1:45 pm	
2:00 pm	
2:15 pm	
2:30 pm	
2:45 pm	
3:00 pm	
3:15 pm	
3:30 pm	
3:45 pm	
4:00 pm	
4:15 pm	
4:30 pm	
4:45 pm	
5:00 pm	
5:15 pm	
5:30 pm	
5:45 pm	
6:00 pm	

TIME MANAGEMENT

PERSONAL DEVELOPMENT	INSPECT	JOB DESCRIPTION	CREATE MAGIC!

Date _____   Date _____   Date _____

THURSDAY	FRIDAY	SATURDAY

THURSDAY

8:00 am	
8:15 am	
8:30 am	
8:45 am	
9:00 am	
9:15 am	
9:30 am	
9:45 am	
10:00 am	
10:15 am	
10:30 am	
10:45 am	
11:00 am	
11:15 am	
11:30 am	
11:45 am	
12:00 pm	
12:15 pm	
12:30 pm	
12:45 pm	
1:00 pm	
1:15 pm	
1:30 pm	
1:45 pm	
2:00 pm	
2:15 pm	
2:30 pm	
2:45 pm	
3:00 pm	
3:15 pm	
3:30 pm	
3:45 pm	
4:00 pm	
4:15 pm	
4:30 pm	
4:45 pm	
5:00 pm	
5:15 pm	
5:30 pm	
5:45 pm	
6:00 pm	

FRIDAY

8:00 am	
8:15 am	
8:30 am	
8:45 am	
9:00 am	
9:15 am	
9:30 am	
9:45 am	
10:00 am	
10:15 am	
10:30 am	
10:45 am	
11:00 am	
11:15 am	
11:30 am	
11:45 am	
12:00 pm	
12:15 pm	
12:30 pm	
12:45 pm	
1:00 pm	
1:15 pm	
1:30 pm	
1:45 pm	
2:00 pm	
2:15 pm	
2:30 pm	
2:45 pm	
3:00 pm	
3:15 pm	
3:30 pm	
3:45 pm	
4:00 pm	
4:15 pm	
4:30 pm	
4:45 pm	
5:00 pm	
5:15 pm	
5:30 pm	
5:45 pm	
6:00 pm	

SATURDAY

SUNDAY

TIME MANAGEMENT

PERSONAL DEVELOPMENT	INSPECT	JOB DESCRIPTION	CREATE MAGIC!

Date _____

MONDAY

8:00 am	
8:15 am	
8:30 am	
8:45 am	
9:00 am	
9:15 am	
9:30 am	
9:45 am	
10:00 am	
10:15 am	
10:30 am	
10:45 am	
11:00 am	
11:15 am	
11:30 am	
11:45 am	
12:00 pm	
12:15 pm	
12:30 pm	
12:45 pm	
1:00 pm	
1:15 pm	
1:30 pm	
1:45 pm	
2:00 pm	
2:15 pm	
2:30 pm	
2:45 pm	
3:00 pm	
3:15 pm	
3:30 pm	
3:45 pm	
4:00 pm	
4:15 pm	
4:30 pm	
4:45 pm	
5:00 pm	
5:15 pm	
5:30 pm	
5:45 pm	
6:00 pm	

Date _____

TUESDAY

8:00 am	
8:15 am	
8:30 am	
8:45 am	
9:00 am	
9:15 am	
9:30 am	
9:45 am	
10:00 am	
10:15 am	
10:30 am	
10:45 am	
11:00 am	
11:15 am	
11:30 am	
11:45 am	
12:00 pm	
12:15 pm	
12:30 pm	
12:45 pm	
1:00 pm	
1:15 pm	
1:30 pm	
1:45 pm	
2:00 pm	
2:15 pm	
2:30 pm	
2:45 pm	
3:00 pm	
3:15 pm	
3:30 pm	
3:45 pm	
4:00 pm	
4:15 pm	
4:30 pm	
4:45 pm	
5:00 pm	
5:15 pm	
5:30 pm	
5:45 pm	
6:00 pm	

Date _____

WEDNESDAY

8:00 am	
8:15 am	
8:30 am	
8:45 am	
9:00 am	
9:15 am	
9:30 am	
9:45 am	
10:00 am	
10:15 am	
10:30 am	
10:45 am	
11:00 am	
11:15 am	
11:30 am	
11:45 am	
12:00 pm	
12:15 pm	
12:30 pm	
12:45 pm	
1:00 pm	
1:15 pm	
1:30 pm	
1:45 pm	
2:00 pm	
2:15 pm	
2:30 pm	
2:45 pm	
3:00 pm	
3:15 pm	
3:30 pm	
3:45 pm	
4:00 pm	
4:15 pm	
4:30 pm	
4:45 pm	
5:00 pm	
5:15 pm	
5:30 pm	
5:45 pm	
6:00 pm	

TIME MANAGEMENT

PERSONAL DEVELOPMENT	INSPECT	JOB DESCRIPTION	CREATE MAGIC!

Date _____   Date _____   Date _____

THURSDAY		FRIDAY		SATURDAY
8:00 am		8:00 am		
8:15 am		8:15 am		
8:30 am		8:30 am		
8:45 am		8:45 am		
9:00 am		9:00 am		
9:15 am		9:15 am		
9:30 am		9:30 am		
9:45 am		9:45 am		
10:00 am		10:00 am		
10:15 am		10:15 am		
10:30 am		10:30 am		
10:45 am		10:45 am		
11:00 am		11:00 am		
11:15 am		11:15 am		
11:30 am		11:30 am		
11:45 am		11:45 am		
12:00 pm		12:00 pm		
12:15 pm		12:15 pm		
12:30 pm		12:30 pm		
12:45 pm		12:45 pm		
1:00 pm		1:00 pm		SUNDAY
1:15 pm		1:15 pm		
1:30 pm		1:30 pm		
1:45 pm		1:45 pm		
2:00 pm		2:00 pm		
2:15 pm		2:15 pm		
2:30 pm		2:30 pm		
2:45 pm		2:45 pm		
3:00 pm		3:00 pm		
3:15 pm		3:15 pm		
3:30 pm		3:30 pm		
3:45 pm		3:45 pm		
4:00 pm		4:00 pm		
4:15 pm		4:15 pm		
4:30 pm		4:30 pm		
4:45 pm		4:45 pm		
5:00 pm		5:00 pm		
5:15 pm		5:15 pm		
5:30 pm		5:30 pm		
5:45 pm		5:45 pm		
6:00 pm		6:00 pm		

TIME MANAGEMENT

PERSONAL DEVELOPMENT	INSPECT	JOB DESCRIPTION	CREATE MAGIC!

53

Date _____   Date _____   Date _____

MONDAY	TUESDAY	WEDNESDAY
8:00 am	8:00 am	8:00 am
8:15 am	8:15 am	8:15 am
8:30 am	8:30 am	8:30 am
8:45 am	8:45 am	8:45 am
9:00 am	9:00 am	9:00 am
9:15 am	9:15 am	9:15 am
9:30 am	9:30 am	9:30 am
9:45 am	9:45 am	9:45 am
10:00 am	10:00 am	10:00 am
10:15 am	10:15 am	10:15 am
10:30 am	10:30 am	10:30 am
10:45 am	10:45 am	10:45 am
11:00 am	11:00 am	11:00 am
11:15 am	11:15 am	11:15 am
11:30 am	11:30 am	11:30 am
11:45 am	11:45 am	11:45 am
12:00 pm	12:00 pm	12:00 pm
12:15 pm	12:15 pm	12:15 pm
12:30 pm	12:30 pm	12:30 pm
12:45 pm	12:45 pm	12:45 pm
1:00 pm	1:00 pm	1:00 pm
1:15 pm	1:15 pm	1:15 pm
1:30 pm	1:30 pm	1:30 pm
1:45 pm	1:45 pm	1:45 pm
2:00 pm	2:00 pm	2:00 pm
2:15 pm	2:15 pm	2:15 pm
2:30 pm	2:30 pm	2:30 pm
2:45 pm	2:45 pm	2:45 pm
3:00 pm	3:00 pm	3:00 pm
3:15 pm	3:15 pm	3:15 pm
3:30 pm	3:30 pm	3:30 pm
3:45 pm	3:45 pm	3:45 pm
4:00 pm	4:00 pm	4:00 pm
4:15 pm	4:15 pm	4:15 pm
4:30 pm	4:30 pm	4:30 pm
4:45 pm	4:45 pm	4:45 pm
5:00 pm	5:00 pm	5:00 pm
5:15 pm	5:15 pm	5:15 pm
5:30 pm	5:30 pm	5:30 pm
5:45 pm	5:45 pm	5:45 pm
6:00 pm	6:00 pm	6:00 pm

TIME MANAGEMENT

PERSONAL DEVELOPMENT	INSPECT	JOB DESCRIPTION	CREATE MAGIC!

Date _____

THURSDAY

8:00 am	
8:15 am	
8:30 am	
8:45 am	
9:00 am	
9:15 am	
9:30 am	
9:45 am	
10:00 am	
10:15 am	
10:30 am	
10:45 am	
11:00 am	
11:15 am	
11:30 am	
11:45 am	
12:00 pm	
12:15 pm	
12:30 pm	
12:45 pm	
1:00 pm	
1:15 pm	
1:30 pm	
1:45 pm	
2:00 pm	
2:15 pm	
2:30 pm	
2:45 pm	
3:00 pm	
3:15 pm	
3:30 pm	
3:45 pm	
4:00 pm	
4:15 pm	
4:30 pm	
4:45 pm	
5:00 pm	
5:15 pm	
5:30 pm	
5:45 pm	
6:00 pm	

Date _____

FRIDAY

8:00 am	
8:15 am	
8:30 am	
8:45 am	
9:00 am	
9:15 am	
9:30 am	
9:45 am	
10:00 am	
10:15 am	
10:30 am	
10:45 am	
11:00 am	
11:15 am	
11:30 am	
11:45 am	
12:00 pm	
12:15 pm	
12:30 pm	
12:45 pm	
1:00 pm	
1:15 pm	
1:30 pm	
1:45 pm	
2:00 pm	
2:15 pm	
2:30 pm	
2:45 pm	
3:00 pm	
3:15 pm	
3:30 pm	
3:45 pm	
4:00 pm	
4:15 pm	
4:30 pm	
4:45 pm	
5:00 pm	
5:15 pm	
5:30 pm	
5:45 pm	
6:00 pm	

Date _____

SATURDAY

SUNDAY

DAILY PLANNER

TIME MANAGEMENT

PERSONAL DEVELOPMENT	INSPECT	JOB DESCRIPTION	CREATE MAGIC!

55

Date _____

Date _____

Date _____

MONDAY	TUESDAY	WEDNESDAY
8:00 am	8:00 am	8:00 am
8:15 am	8:15 am	8:15 am
8:30 am	8:30 am	8:30 am
8:45 am	8:45 am	8:45 am
9:00 am	9:00 am	9:00 am
9:15 am	9:15 am	9:15 am
9:30 am	9:30 am	9:30 am
9:45 am	9:45 am	9:45 am
10:00 am	10:00 am	10:00 am
10:15 am	10:15 am	10:15 am
10:30 am	10:30 am	10:30 am
10:45 am	10:45 am	10:45 am
11:00 am	11:00 am	11:00 am
11:15 am	11:15 am	11:15 am
11:30 am	11:30 am	11:30 am
11:45 am	11:45 am	11:45 am
12:00 pm	12:00 pm	12:00 pm
12:15 pm	12:15 pm	12:15 pm
12:30 pm	12:30 pm	12:30 pm
12:45 pm	12:45 pm	12:45 pm
1:00 pm	1:00 pm	1:00 pm
1:15 pm	1:15 pm	1:15 pm
1:30 pm	1:30 pm	1:30 pm
1:45 pm	1:45 pm	1:45 pm
2:00 pm	2:00 pm	2:00 pm
2:15 pm	2:15 pm	2:15 pm
2:30 pm	2:30 pm	2:30 pm
2:45 pm	2:45 pm	2:45 pm
3:00 pm	3:00 pm	3:00 pm
3:15 pm	3:15 pm	3:15 pm
3:30 pm	3:30 pm	3:30 pm
3:45 pm	3:45 pm	3:45 pm
4:00 pm	4:00 pm	4:00 pm
4:15 pm	4:15 pm	4:15 pm
4:30 pm	4:30 pm	4:30 pm
4:45 pm	4:45 pm	4:45 pm
5:00 pm	5:00 pm	5:00 pm
5:15 pm	5:15 pm	5:15 pm
5:30 pm	5:30 pm	5:30 pm
5:45 pm	5:45 pm	5:45 pm
6:00 pm	6:00 pm	6:00 pm

TIME MANAGEMENT

PERSONAL DEVELOPMENT	INSPECT	JOB DESCRIPTION	CREATE MAGIC!

Date _____   Date _____   Date _____

THURSDAY	FRIDAY	SATURDAY
8:00 am	8:00 am	
8:15 am	8:15 am	
8:30 am	8:30 am	
8:45 am	8:45 am	
9:00 am	9:00 am	
9:15 am	9:15 am	
9:30 am	9:30 am	
9:45 am	9:45 am	
10:00 am	10:00 am	
10:15 am	10:15 am	
10:30 am	10:30 am	
10:45 am	10:45 am	
11:00 am	11:00 am	
11:15 am	11:15 am	
11:30 am	11:30 am	
11:45 am	11:45 am	
12:00 pm	12:00 pm	
12:15 pm	12:15 pm	
12:30 pm	12:30 pm	
12:45 pm	12:45 pm	
1:00 pm	1:00 pm	

		SUNDAY
1:15 pm	1:15 pm	
1:30 pm	1:30 pm	
1:45 pm	1:45 pm	
2:00 pm	2:00 pm	
2:15 pm	2:15 pm	
2:30 pm	2:30 pm	
2:45 pm	2:45 pm	
3:00 pm	3:00 pm	
3:15 pm	3:15 pm	
3:30 pm	3:30 pm	
3:45 pm	3:45 pm	
4:00 pm	4:00 pm	
4:15 pm	4:15 pm	
4:30 pm	4:30 pm	
4:45 pm	4:45 pm	
5:00 pm	5:00 pm	
5:15 pm	5:15 pm	
5:30 pm	5:30 pm	
5:45 pm	5:45 pm	
6:00 pm	6:00 pm	

TIME MANAGEMENT

PERSONAL DEVELOPMENT	INSPECT	JOB DESCRIPTION	CREATE MAGIC!

Date _____

MONDAY

8:00 am	
8:15 am	
8:30 am	
8:45 am	
9:00 am	
9:15 am	
9:30 am	
9:45 am	
10:00 am	
10:15 am	
10:30 am	
10:45 am	
11:00 am	
11:15 am	
11:30 am	
11:45 am	
12:00 pm	
12:15 pm	
12:30 pm	
12:45 pm	
1:00 pm	
1:15 pm	
1:30 pm	
1:45 pm	
2:00 pm	
2:15 pm	
2:30 pm	
2:45 pm	
3:00 pm	
3:15 pm	
3:30 pm	
3:45 pm	
4:00 pm	
4:15 pm	
4:30 pm	
4:45 pm	
5:00 pm	
5:15 pm	
5:30 pm	
5:45 pm	
6:00 pm	

Date _____

TUESDAY

8:00 am	
8:15 am	
8:30 am	
8:45 am	
9:00 am	
9:15 am	
9:30 am	
9:45 am	
10:00 am	
10:15 am	
10:30 am	
10:45 am	
11:00 am	
11:15 am	
11:30 am	
11:45 am	
12:00 pm	
12:15 pm	
12:30 pm	
12:45 pm	
1:00 pm	
1:15 pm	
1:30 pm	
1:45 pm	
2:00 pm	
2:15 pm	
2:30 pm	
2:45 pm	
3:00 pm	
3:15 pm	
3:30 pm	
3:45 pm	
4:00 pm	
4:15 pm	
4:30 pm	
4:45 pm	
5:00 pm	
5:15 pm	
5:30 pm	
5:45 pm	
6:00 pm	

Date _____

WEDNESDAY

8:00 am	
8:15 am	
8:30 am	
8:45 am	
9:00 am	
9:15 am	
9:30 am	
9:45 am	
10:00 am	
10:15 am	
10:30 am	
10:45 am	
11:00 am	
11:15 am	
11:30 am	
11:45 am	
12:00 pm	
12:15 pm	
12:30 pm	
12:45 pm	
1:00 pm	
1:15 pm	
1:30 pm	
1:45 pm	
2:00 pm	
2:15 pm	
2:30 pm	
2:45 pm	
3:00 pm	
3:15 pm	
3:30 pm	
3:45 pm	
4:00 pm	
4:15 pm	
4:30 pm	
4:45 pm	
5:00 pm	
5:15 pm	
5:30 pm	
5:45 pm	
6:00 pm	

TIME MANAGEMENT

PERSONAL DEVELOPMENT	INSPECT	JOB DESCRIPTION	CREATE MAGIC!

Date _____   Date _____   Date _____

THURSDAY	FRIDAY	SATURDAY
8:00 am	8:00 am	
8:15 am	8:15 am	
8:30 am	8:30 am	
8:45 am	8:45 am	
9:00 am	9:00 am	
9:15 am	9:15 am	
9:30 am	9:30 am	
9:45 am	9:45 am	
10:00 am	10:00 am	
10:15 am	10:15 am	
10:30 am	10:30 am	
10:45 am	10:45 am	
11:00 am	11:00 am	
11:15 am	11:15 am	
11:30 am	11:30 am	
11:45 am	11:45 am	
12:00 pm	12:00 pm	
12:15 pm	12:15 pm	
12:30 pm	12:30 pm	
12:45 pm	12:45 pm	
1:00 pm	1:00 pm	

THURSDAY	FRIDAY	SUNDAY
1:15 pm	1:15 pm	
1:30 pm	1:30 pm	
1:45 pm	1:45 pm	
2:00 pm	2:00 pm	
2:15 pm	2:15 pm	
2:30 pm	2:30 pm	
2:45 pm	2:45 pm	
3:00 pm	3:00 pm	
3:15 pm	3:15 pm	
3:30 pm	3:30 pm	
3:45 pm	3:45 pm	
4:00 pm	4:00 pm	
4:15 pm	4:15 pm	
4:30 pm	4:30 pm	
4:45 pm	4:45 pm	
5:00 pm	5:00 pm	
5:15 pm	5:15 pm	
5:30 pm	5:30 pm	
5:45 pm	5:45 pm	
6:00 pm	6:00 pm	

TIME MANAGEMENT

PERSONAL DEVELOPMENT	INSPECT	JOB DESCRIPTION	CREATE MAGIC!

Date _____

MONDAY

8:00 am	
8:15 am	
8:30 am	
8:45 am	
9:00 am	
9:15 am	
9:30 am	
9:45 am	
10:00 am	
10:15 am	
10:30 am	
10:45 am	
11:00 am	
11:15 am	
11:30 am	
11:45 am	
12:00 pm	
12:15 pm	
12:30 pm	
12:45 pm	
1:00 pm	
1:15 pm	
1:30 pm	
1:45 pm	
2:00 pm	
2:15 pm	
2:30 pm	
2:45 pm	
3:00 pm	
3:15 pm	
3:30 pm	
3:45 pm	
4:00 pm	
4:15 pm	
4:30 pm	
4:45 pm	
5:00 pm	
5:15 pm	
5:30 pm	
5:45 pm	
6:00 pm	

Date _____

TUESDAY

8:00 am	
8:15 am	
8:30 am	
8:45 am	
9:00 am	
9:15 am	
9:30 am	
9:45 am	
10:00 am	
10:15 am	
10:30 am	
10:45 am	
11:00 am	
11:15 am	
11:30 am	
11:45 am	
12:00 pm	
12:15 pm	
12:30 pm	
12:45 pm	
1:00 pm	
1:15 pm	
1:30 pm	
1:45 pm	
2:00 pm	
2:15 pm	
2:30 pm	
2:45 pm	
3:00 pm	
3:15 pm	
3:30 pm	
3:45 pm	
4:00 pm	
4:15 pm	
4:30 pm	
4:45 pm	
5:00 pm	
5:15 pm	
5:30 pm	
5:45 pm	
6:00 pm	

Date _____

WEDNESDAY

8:00 am	
8:15 am	
8:30 am	
8:45 am	
9:00 am	
9:15 am	
9:30 am	
9:45 am	
10:00 am	
10:15 am	
10:30 am	
10:45 am	
11:00 am	
11:15 am	
11:30 am	
11:45 am	
12:00 pm	
12:15 pm	
12:30 pm	
12:45 pm	
1:00 pm	
1:15 pm	
1:30 pm	
1:45 pm	
2:00 pm	
2:15 pm	
2:30 pm	
2:45 pm	
3:00 pm	
3:15 pm	
3:30 pm	
3:45 pm	
4:00 pm	
4:15 pm	
4:30 pm	
4:45 pm	
5:00 pm	
5:15 pm	
5:30 pm	
5:45 pm	
6:00 pm	

TIME MANAGEMENT

PERSONAL DEVELOPMENT	INSPECT	JOB DESCRIPTION	CREATE MAGIC!

Date _____ Date _____ Date _____

THURSDAY	FRIDAY	SATURDAY

THURSDAY	FRIDAY	SATURDAY
8:00 am	8:00 am	
8:15 am	8:15 am	
8:30 am	8:30 am	
8:45 am	8:45 am	
9:00 am	9:00 am	
9:15 am	9:15 am	
9:30 am	9:30 am	
9:45 am	9:45 am	
10:00 am	10:00 am	
10:15 am	10:15 am	
10:30 am	10:30 am	
10:45 am	10:45 am	
11:00 am	11:00 am	
11:15 am	11:15 am	
11:30 am	11:30 am	
11:45 am	11:45 am	
12:00 pm	12:00 pm	
12:15 pm	12:15 pm	
12:30 pm	12:30 pm	
12:45 pm	12:45 pm	

SUNDAY

THURSDAY	FRIDAY	SUNDAY
1:00 pm	1:00 pm	
1:15 pm	1:15 pm	
1:30 pm	1:30 pm	
1:45 pm	1:45 pm	
2:00 pm	2:00 pm	
2:15 pm	2:15 pm	
2:30 pm	2:30 pm	
2:45 pm	2:45 pm	
3:00 pm	3:00 pm	
3:15 pm	3:15 pm	
3:30 pm	3:30 pm	
3:45 pm	3:45 pm	
4:00 pm	4:00 pm	
4:15 pm	4:15 pm	
4:30 pm	4:30 pm	
4:45 pm	4:45 pm	
5:00 pm	5:00 pm	
5:15 pm	5:15 pm	
5:30 pm	5:30 pm	
5:45 pm	5:45 pm	
6:00 pm	6:00 pm	

TIME MANAGEMENT

PERSONAL DEVELOPMENT	INSPECT	JOB DESCRIPTION	CREATE MAGIC!

Date _____   Date _____   Date _____

MONDAY	TUESDAY	WEDNESDAY
8:00 am	8:00 am	8:00 am
8:15 am	8:15 am	8:15 am
8:30 am	8:30 am	8:30 am
8:45 am	8:45 am	8:45 am
9:00 am	9:00 am	9:00 am
9:15 am	9:15 am	9:15 am
9:30 am	9:30 am	9:30 am
9:45 am	9:45 am	9:45 am
10:00 am	10:00 am	10:00 am
10:15 am	10:15 am	10:15 am
10:30 am	10:30 am	10:30 am
10:45 am	10:45 am	10:45 am
11:00 am	11:00 am	11:00 am
11:15 am	11:15 am	11:15 am
11:30 am	11:30 am	11:30 am
11:45 am	11:45 am	11:45 am
12:00 pm	12:00 pm	12:00 pm
12:15 pm	12:15 pm	12:15 pm
12:30 pm	12:30 pm	12:30 pm
12:45 pm	12:45 pm	12:45 pm
1:00 pm	1:00 pm	1:00 pm
1:15 pm	1:15 pm	1:15 pm
1:30 pm	1:30 pm	1:30 pm
1:45 pm	1:45 pm	1:45 pm
2:00 pm	2:00 pm	2:00 pm
2:15 pm	2:15 pm	2:15 pm
2:30 pm	2:30 pm	2:30 pm
2:45 pm	2:45 pm	2:45 pm
3:00 pm	3:00 pm	3:00 pm
3:15 pm	3:15 pm	3:15 pm
3:30 pm	3:30 pm	3:30 pm
3:45 pm	3:45 pm	3:45 pm
4:00 pm	4:00 pm	4:00 pm
4:15 pm	4:15 pm	4:15 pm
4:30 pm	4:30 pm	4:30 pm
4:45 pm	4:45 pm	4:45 pm
5:00 pm	5:00 pm	5:00 pm
5:15 pm	5:15 pm	5:15 pm
5:30 pm	5:30 pm	5:30 pm
5:45 pm	5:45 pm	5:45 pm
6:00 pm	6:00 pm	6:00 pm

TIME MANAGEMENT

PERSONAL DEVELOPMENT	INSPECT	JOB DESCRIPTION	CREATE MAGIC!

Date _____   Date _____   Date _____

THURSDAY	FRIDAY	SATURDAY

THURSDAY

8:00 am
8:15 am
8:30 am
8:45 am
9:00 am
9:15 am
9:30 am
9:45 am
10:00 am
10:15 am
10:30 am
10:45 am
11:00 am
11:15 am
11:30 am
11:45 am
12:00 pm
12:15 pm
12:30 pm
12:45 pm
1:00 pm
1:15 pm
1:30 pm
1:45 pm
2:00 pm
2:15 pm
2:30 pm
2:45 pm
3:00 pm
3:15 pm
3:30 pm
3:45 pm
4:00 pm
4:15 pm
4:30 pm
4:45 pm
5:00 pm
5:15 pm
5:30 pm
5:45 pm
6:00 pm

FRIDAY

8:00 am
8:15 am
8:30 am
8:45 am
9:00 am
9:15 am
9:30 am
9:45 am
10:00 am
10:15 am
10:30 am
10:45 am
11:00 am
11:15 am
11:30 am
11:45 am
12:00 pm
12:15 pm
12:30 pm
12:45 pm
1:00 pm
1:15 pm
1:30 pm
1:45 pm
2:00 pm
2:15 pm
2:30 pm
2:45 pm
3:00 pm
3:15 pm
3:30 pm
3:45 pm
4:00 pm
4:15 pm
4:30 pm
4:45 pm
5:00 pm
5:15 pm
5:30 pm
5:45 pm
6:00 pm

SATURDAY

SUNDAY

TIME MANAGEMENT			
PERSONAL DEVELOPMENT	INSPECT	JOB DESCRIPTION	CREATE MAGIC!

Date _____   Date _____   Date _____

MONDAY		**TUESDAY**		**WEDNESDAY**
8:00 am		8:00 am		8:00 am
8:15 am		8:15 am		8:15 am
8:30 am		8:30 am		8:30 am
8:45 am		8:45 am		8:45 am
9:00 am		9:00 am		9:00 am
9:15 am		9:15 am		9:15 am
9:30 am		9:30 am		9:30 am
9:45 am		9:45 am		9:45 am
10:00 am		10:00 am		10:00 am
10:15 am		10:15 am		10:15 am
10:30 am		10:30 am		10:30 am
10:45 am		10:45 am		10:45 am
11:00 am		11:00 am		11:00 am
11:15 am		11:15 am		11:15 am
11:30 am		11:30 am		11:30 am
11:45 am		11:45 am		11:45 am
12:00 pm		12:00 pm		12:00 pm
12:15 pm		12:15 pm		12:15 pm
12:30 pm		12:30 pm		12:30 pm
12:45 pm		12:45 pm		12:45 pm
1:00 pm		1:00 pm		1:00 pm
1:15 pm		1:15 pm		1:15 pm
1:30 pm		1:30 pm		1:30 pm
1:45 pm		1:45 pm		1:45 pm
2:00 pm		2:00 pm		2:00 pm
2:15 pm		2:15 pm		2:15 pm
2:30 pm		2:30 pm		2:30 pm
2:45 pm		2:45 pm		2:45 pm
3:00 pm		3:00 pm		3:00 pm
3:15 pm		3:15 pm		3:15 pm
3:30 pm		3:30 pm		3:30 pm
3:45 pm		3:45 pm		3:45 pm
4:00 pm		4:00 pm		4:00 pm
4:15 pm		4:15 pm		4:15 pm
4:30 pm		4:30 pm		4:30 pm
4:45 pm		4:45 pm		4:45 pm
5:00 pm		5:00 pm		5:00 pm
5:15 pm		5:15 pm		5:15 pm
5:30 pm		5:30 pm		5:30 pm
5:45 pm		5:45 pm		5:45 pm
6:00 pm		6:00 pm		6:00 pm

TIME MANAGEMENT

PERSONAL DEVELOPMENT	INSPECT	JOB DESCRIPTION	CREATE MAGIC!

Date _____ Date _____ Date _____

THURSDAY		FRIDAY		SATURDAY
8:00 am		8:00 am		
8:15 am		8:15 am		
8:30 am		8:30 am		
8:45 am		8:45 am		
9:00 am		9:00 am		
9:15 am		9:15 am		
9:30 am		9:30 am		
9:45 am		9:45 am		
10:00 am		10:00 am		
10:15 am		10:15 am		
10:30 am		10:30 am		
10:45 am		10:45 am		
11:00 am		11:00 am		
11:15 am		11:15 am		
11:30 am		11:30 am		
11:45 am		11:45 am		
12:00 pm		12:00 pm		
12:15 pm		12:15 pm		
12:30 pm		12:30 pm		
12:45 pm		12:45 pm		

				SUNDAY
1:00 pm		1:00 pm		
1:15 pm		1:15 pm		
1:30 pm		1:30 pm		
1:45 pm		1:45 pm		
2:00 pm		2:00 pm		
2:15 pm		2:15 pm		
2:30 pm		2:30 pm		
2:45 pm		2:45 pm		
3:00 pm		3:00 pm		
3:15 pm		3:15 pm		
3:30 pm		3:30 pm		
3:45 pm		3:45 pm		
4:00 pm		4:00 pm		
4:15 pm		4:15 pm		
4:30 pm		4:30 pm		
4:45 pm		4:45 pm		
5:00 pm		5:00 pm		
5:15 pm		5:15 pm		
5:30 pm		5:30 pm		
5:45 pm		5:45 pm		
6:00 pm		6:00 pm		

TIME MANAGEMENT

PERSONAL DEVELOPMENT	INSPECT	JOB DESCRIPTION	CREATE MAGIC!

65

Date _____	Date _____	Date _____
MONDAY	**TUESDAY**	**WEDNESDAY**

MONDAY	TUESDAY	WEDNESDAY
8:00 am	8:00 am	8:00 am
8:15 am	8:15 am	8:15 am
8:30 am	8:30 am	8:30 am
8:45 am	8:45 am	8:45 am
9:00 am	9:00 am	9:00 am
9:15 am	9:15 am	9:15 am
9:30 am	9:30 am	9:30 am
9:45 am	9:45 am	9:45 am
10:00 am	10:00 am	10:00 am
10:15 am	10:15 am	10:15 am
10:30 am	10:30 am	10:30 am
10:45 am	10:45 am	10:45 am
11:00 am	11:00 am	11:00 am
11:15 am	11:15 am	11:15 am
11:30 am	11:30 am	11:30 am
11:45 am	11:45 am	11:45 am
12:00 pm	12:00 pm	12:00 pm
12:15 pm	12:15 pm	12:15 pm
12:30 pm	12:30 pm	12:30 pm
12:45 pm	12:45 pm	12:45 pm
1:00 pm	1:00 pm	1:00 pm
1:15 pm	1:15 pm	1:15 pm
1:30 pm	1:30 pm	1:30 pm
1:45 pm	1:45 pm	1:45 pm
2:00 pm	2:00 pm	2:00 pm
2:15 pm	2:15 pm	2:15 pm
2:30 pm	2:30 pm	2:30 pm
2:45 pm	2:45 pm	2:45 pm
3:00 pm	3:00 pm	3:00 pm
3:15 pm	3:15 pm	3:15 pm
3:30 pm	3:30 pm	3:30 pm
3:45 pm	3:45 pm	3:45 pm
4:00 pm	4:00 pm	4:00 pm
4:15 pm	4:15 pm	4:15 pm
4:30 pm	4:30 pm	4:30 pm
4:45 pm	4:45 pm	4:45 pm
5:00 pm	5:00 pm	5:00 pm
5:15 pm	5:15 pm	5:15 pm
5:30 pm	5:30 pm	5:30 pm
5:45 pm	5:45 pm	5:45 pm
6:00 pm	6:00 pm	6:00 pm

TIME MANAGEMENT

PERSONAL DEVELOPMENT	INSPECT	JOB DESCRIPTION	CREATE MAGIC!

Date _____ Date _____ Date _____

THURSDAY		FRIDAY		SATURDAY	
8:00 am		8:00 am			
8:15 am		8:15 am			
8:30 am		8:30 am			
8:45 am		8:45 am			
9:00 am		9:00 am			
9:15 am		9:15 am			
9:30 am		9:30 am			
9:45 am		9:45 am			
10:00 am		10:00 am			
10:15 am		10:15 am			
10:30 am		10:30 am			
10:45 am		10:45 am			
11:00 am		11:00 am			
11:15 am		11:15 am			
11:30 am		11:30 am			
11:45 am		11:45 am			
12:00 pm		12:00 pm			
12:15 pm		12:15 pm			
12:30 pm		12:30 pm			
12:45 pm		12:45 pm			
1:00 pm		1:00 pm		SUNDAY	
1:15 pm		1:15 pm			
1:30 pm		1:30 pm			
1:45 pm		1:45 pm			
2:00 pm		2:00 pm			
2:15 pm		2:15 pm			
2:30 pm		2:30 pm			
2:45 pm		2:45 pm			
3:00 pm		3:00 pm			
3:15 pm		3:15 pm			
3:30 pm		3:30 pm			
3:45 pm		3:45 pm			
4:00 pm		4:00 pm			
4:15 pm		4:15 pm			
4:30 pm		4:30 pm			
4:45 pm		4:45 pm			
5:00 pm		5:00 pm			
5:15 pm		5:15 pm			
5:30 pm		5:30 pm			
5:45 pm		5:45 pm			
6:00 pm		6:00 pm			

TIME MANAGEMENT

PERSONAL DEVELOPMENT	INSPECT	JOB DESCRIPTION	CREATE MAGIC!

Date _____

Date _____

Date _____

MONDAY	TUESDAY	WEDNESDAY
8:00 am	8:00 am	8:00 am
8:15 am	8:15 am	8:15 am
8:30 am	8:30 am	8:30 am
8:45 am	8:45 am	8:45 am
9:00 am	9:00 am	9:00 am
9:15 am	9:15 am	9:15 am
9:30 am	9:30 am	9:30 am
9:45 am	9:45 am	9:45 am
10:00 am	10:00 am	10:00 am
10:15 am	10:15 am	10:15 am
10:30 am	10:30 am	10:30 am
10:45 am	10:45 am	10:45 am
11:00 am	11:00 am	11:00 am
11:15 am	11:15 am	11:15 am
11:30 am	11:30 am	11:30 am
11:45 am	11:45 am	11:45 am
12:00 pm	12:00 pm	12:00 pm
12:15 pm	12:15 pm	12:15 pm
12:30 pm	12:30 pm	12:30 pm
12:45 pm	12:45 pm	12:45 pm
1:00 pm	1:00 pm	1:00 pm
1:15 pm	1:15 pm	1:15 pm
1:30 pm	1:30 pm	1:30 pm
1:45 pm	1:45 pm	1:45 pm
2:00 pm	2:00 pm	2:00 pm
2:15 pm	2:15 pm	2:15 pm
2:30 pm	2:30 pm	2:30 pm
2:45 pm	2:45 pm	2:45 pm
3:00 pm	3:00 pm	3:00 pm
3:15 pm	3:15 pm	3:15 pm
3:30 pm	3:30 pm	3:30 pm
3:45 pm	3:45 pm	3:45 pm
4:00 pm	4:00 pm	4:00 pm
4:15 pm	4:15 pm	4:15 pm
4:30 pm	4:30 pm	4:30 pm
4:45 pm	4:45 pm	4:45 pm
5:00 pm	5:00 pm	5:00 pm
5:15 pm	5:15 pm	5:15 pm
5:30 pm	5:30 pm	5:30 pm
5:45 pm	5:45 pm	5:45 pm
6:00 pm	6:00 pm	6:00 pm

TIME MANAGEMENT

PERSONAL DEVELOPMENT	INSPECT	JOB DESCRIPTION	CREATE MAGIC!

Date _____   Date _____   Date _____

THURSDAY		FRIDAY		SATURDAY

THURSDAY

8:00 am	
8:15 am	
8:30 am	
8:45 am	
9:00 am	
9:15 am	
9:30 am	
9:45 am	
10:00 am	
10:15 am	
10:30 am	
10:45 am	
11:00 am	
11:15 am	
11:30 am	
11:45 am	
12:00 pm	
12:15 pm	
12:30 pm	
12:45 pm	
1:00 pm	
1:15 pm	
1:30 pm	
1:45 pm	
2:00 pm	
2:15 pm	
2:30 pm	
2:45 pm	
3:00 pm	
3:15 pm	
3:30 pm	
3:45 pm	
4:00 pm	
4:15 pm	
4:30 pm	
4:45 pm	
5:00 pm	
5:15 pm	
5:30 pm	
5:45 pm	
6:00 pm	

FRIDAY

8:00 am	
8:15 am	
8:30 am	
8:45 am	
9:00 am	
9:15 am	
9:30 am	
9:45 am	
10:00 am	
10:15 am	
10:30 am	
10:45 am	
11:00 am	
11:15 am	
11:30 am	
11:45 am	
12:00 pm	
12:15 pm	
12:30 pm	
12:45 pm	
1:00 pm	
1:15 pm	
1:30 pm	
1:45 pm	
2:00 pm	
2:15 pm	
2:30 pm	
2:45 pm	
3:00 pm	
3:15 pm	
3:30 pm	
3:45 pm	
4:00 pm	
4:15 pm	
4:30 pm	
4:45 pm	
5:00 pm	
5:15 pm	
5:30 pm	
5:45 pm	
6:00 pm	

SATURDAY

SUNDAY

TIME MANAGEMENT

PERSONAL DEVELOPMENT	INSPECT	JOB DESCRIPTION	CREATE MAGIC!

Date _____

Date _____

Date _____

MONDAY	TUESDAY	WEDNESDAY
8:00 am	8:00 am	8:00 am
8:15 am	8:15 am	8:15 am
8:30 am	8:30 am	8:30 am
8:45 am	8:45 am	8:45 am
9:00 am	9:00 am	9:00 am
9:15 am	9:15 am	9:15 am
9:30 am	9:30 am	9:30 am
9:45 am	9:45 am	9:45 am
10:00 am	10:00 am	10:00 am
10:15 am	10:15 am	10:15 am
10:30 am	10:30 am	10:30 am
10:45 am	10:45 am	10:45 am
11:00 am	11:00 am	11:00 am
11:15 am	11:15 am	11:15 am
11:30 am	11:30 am	11:30 am
11:45 am	11:45 am	11:45 am
12:00 pm	12:00 pm	12:00 pm
12:15 pm	12:15 pm	12:15 pm
12:30 pm	12:30 pm	12:30 pm
12:45 pm	12:45 pm	12:45 pm
1:00 pm	1:00 pm	1:00 pm
1:15 pm	1:15 pm	1:15 pm
1:30 pm	1:30 pm	1:30 pm
1:45 pm	1:45 pm	1:45 pm
2:00 pm	2:00 pm	2:00 pm
2:15 pm	2:15 pm	2:15 pm
2:30 pm	2:30 pm	2:30 pm
2:45 pm	2:45 pm	2:45 pm
3:00 pm	3:00 pm	3:00 pm
3:15 pm	3:15 pm	3:15 pm
3:30 pm	3:30 pm	3:30 pm
3:45 pm	3:45 pm	3:45 pm
4:00 pm	4:00 pm	4:00 pm
4:15 pm	4:15 pm	4:15 pm
4:30 pm	4:30 pm	4:30 pm
4:45 pm	4:45 pm	4:45 pm
5:00 pm	5:00 pm	5:00 pm
5:15 pm	5:15 pm	5:15 pm
5:30 pm	5:30 pm	5:30 pm
5:45 pm	5:45 pm	5:45 pm
6:00 pm	6:00 pm	6:00 pm

TIME MANAGEMENT

PERSONAL DEVELOPMENT	INSPECT	JOB DESCRIPTION	CREATE MAGIC!

Date _____   Date _____   Date _____

THURSDAY	FRIDAY	SATURDAY
8:00 am	8:00 am	
8:15 am	8:15 am	
8:30 am	8:30 am	
8:45 am	8:45 am	
9:00 am	9:00 am	
9:15 am	9:15 am	
9:30 am	9:30 am	
9:45 am	9:45 am	
10:00 am	10:00 am	
10:15 am	10:15 am	
10:30 am	10:30 am	
10:45 am	10:45 am	
11:00 am	11:00 am	
11:15 am	11:15 am	
11:30 am	11:30 am	
11:45 am	11:45 am	
12:00 pm	12:00 pm	
12:15 pm	12:15 pm	
12:30 pm	12:30 pm	
12:45 pm	12:45 pm	
1:00 pm	1:00 pm	SUNDAY
1:15 pm	1:15 pm	
1:30 pm	1:30 pm	
1:45 pm	1:45 pm	
2:00 pm	2:00 pm	
2:15 pm	2:15 pm	
2:30 pm	2:30 pm	
2:45 pm	2:45 pm	
3:00 pm	3:00 pm	
3:15 pm	3:15 pm	
3:30 pm	3:30 pm	
3:45 pm	3:45 pm	
4:00 pm	4:00 pm	
4:15 pm	4:15 pm	
4:30 pm	4:30 pm	
4:45 pm	4:45 pm	
5:00 pm	5:00 pm	
5:15 pm	5:15 pm	
5:30 pm	5:30 pm	
5:45 pm	5:45 pm	
6:00 pm	6:00 pm	

TIME MANAGEMENT

PERSONAL DEVELOPMENT	INSPECT	JOB DESCRIPTION	CREATE MAGIC!

Date _____ Date _____ Date _____

MONDAY	TUESDAY	WEDNESDAY
8:00 am	8:00 am	8:00 am
8:15 am	8:15 am	8:15 am
8:30 am	8:30 am	8:30 am
8:45 am	8:45 am	8:45 am
9:00 am	9:00 am	9:00 am
9:15 am	9:15 am	9:15 am
9:30 am	9:30 am	9:30 am
9:45 am	9:45 am	9:45 am
10:00 am	10:00 am	10:00 am
10:15 am	10:15 am	10:15 am
10:30 am	10:30 am	10:30 am
10:45 am	10:45 am	10:45 am
11:00 am	11:00 am	11:00 am
11:15 am	11:15 am	11:15 am
11:30 am	11:30 am	11:30 am
11:45 am	11:45 am	11:45 am
12:00 pm	12:00 pm	12:00 pm
12:15 pm	12:15 pm	12:15 pm
12:30 pm	12:30 pm	12:30 pm
12:45 pm	12:45 pm	12:45 pm
1:00 pm	1:00 pm	1:00 pm
1:15 pm	1:15 pm	1:15 pm
1:30 pm	1:30 pm	1:30 pm
1:45 pm	1:45 pm	1:45 pm
2:00 pm	2:00 pm	2:00 pm
2:15 pm	2:15 pm	2:15 pm
2:30 pm	2:30 pm	2:30 pm
2:45 pm	2:45 pm	2:45 pm
3:00 pm	3:00 pm	3:00 pm
3:15 pm	3:15 pm	3:15 pm
3:30 pm	3:30 pm	3:30 pm
3:45 pm	3:45 pm	3:45 pm
4:00 pm	4:00 pm	4:00 pm
4:15 pm	4:15 pm	4:15 pm
4:30 pm	4:30 pm	4:30 pm
4:45 pm	4:45 pm	4:45 pm
5:00 pm	5:00 pm	5:00 pm
5:15 pm	5:15 pm	5:15 pm
5:30 pm	5:30 pm	5:30 pm
5:45 pm	5:45 pm	5:45 pm
6:00 pm	6:00 pm	6:00 pm

TIME MANAGEMENT

PERSONAL DEVELOPMENT	INSPECT	JOB DESCRIPTION	CREATE MAGIC!

Date _____   Date _____   Date _____

THURSDAY		FRIDAY		SATURDAY
8:00 am		8:00 am		
8:15 am		8:15 am		
8:30 am		8:30 am		
8:45 am		8:45 am		
9:00 am		9:00 am		
9:15 am		9:15 am		
9:30 am		9:30 am		
9:45 am		9:45 am		
10:00 am		10:00 am		
10:15 am		10:15 am		
10:30 am		10:30 am		
10:45 am		10:45 am		
11:00 am		11:00 am		
11:15 am		11:15 am		
11:30 am		11:30 am		
11:45 am		11:45 am		
12:00 pm		12:00 pm		
12:15 pm		12:15 pm		
12:30 pm		12:30 pm		
12:45 pm		12:45 pm		
1:00 pm		1:00 pm		SUNDAY
1:15 pm		1:15 pm		
1:30 pm		1:30 pm		
1:45 pm		1:45 pm		
2:00 pm		2:00 pm		
2:15 pm		2:15 pm		
2:30 pm		2:30 pm		
2:45 pm		2:45 pm		
3:00 pm		3:00 pm		
3:15 pm		3:15 pm		
3:30 pm		3:30 pm		
3:45 pm		3:45 pm		
4:00 pm		4:00 pm		
4:15 pm		4:15 pm		
4:30 pm		4:30 pm		
4:45 pm		4:45 pm		
5:00 pm		5:00 pm		
5:15 pm		5:15 pm		
5:30 pm		5:30 pm		
5:45 pm		5:45 pm		
6:00 pm		6:00 pm		

TIME MANAGEMENT

PERSONAL DEVELOPMENT	INSPECT	JOB DESCRIPTION	CREATE MAGIC!

Date _____

MONDAY

8:00 am	
8:15 am	
8:30 am	
8:45 am	
9:00 am	
9:15 am	
9:30 am	
9:45 am	
10:00 am	
10:15 am	
10:30 am	
10:45 am	
11:00 am	
11:15 am	
11:30 am	
11:45 am	
12:00 pm	
12:15 pm	
12:30 pm	
12:45 pm	
1:00 pm	
1:15 pm	
1:30 pm	
1:45 pm	
2:00 pm	
2:15 pm	
2:30 pm	
2:45 pm	
3:00 pm	
3:15 pm	
3:30 pm	
3:45 pm	
4:00 pm	
4:15 pm	
4:30 pm	
4:45 pm	
5:00 pm	
5:15 pm	
5:30 pm	
5:45 pm	
6:00 pm	

Date _____

TUESDAY

8:00 am	
8:15 am	
8:30 am	
8:45 am	
9:00 am	
9:15 am	
9:30 am	
9:45 am	
10:00 am	
10:15 am	
10:30 am	
10:45 am	
11:00 am	
11:15 am	
11:30 am	
11:45 am	
12:00 pm	
12:15 pm	
12:30 pm	
12:45 pm	
1:00 pm	
1:15 pm	
1:30 pm	
1:45 pm	
2:00 pm	
2:15 pm	
2:30 pm	
2:45 pm	
3:00 pm	
3:15 pm	
3:30 pm	
3:45 pm	
4:00 pm	
4:15 pm	
4:30 pm	
4:45 pm	
5:00 pm	
5:15 pm	
5:30 pm	
5:45 pm	
6:00 pm	

Date _____

WEDNESDAY

8:00 am	
8:15 am	
8:30 am	
8:45 am	
9:00 am	
9:15 am	
9:30 am	
9:45 am	
10:00 am	
10:15 am	
10:30 am	
10:45 am	
11:00 am	
11:15 am	
11:30 am	
11:45 am	
12:00 pm	
12:15 pm	
12:30 pm	
12:45 pm	
1:00 pm	
1:15 pm	
1:30 pm	
1:45 pm	
2:00 pm	
2:15 pm	
2:30 pm	
2:45 pm	
3:00 pm	
3:15 pm	
3:30 pm	
3:45 pm	
4:00 pm	
4:15 pm	
4:30 pm	
4:45 pm	
5:00 pm	
5:15 pm	
5:30 pm	
5:45 pm	
6:00 pm	

TIME MANAGEMENT

PERSONAL DEVELOPMENT	INSPECT	JOB DESCRIPTION	CREATE MAGIC!

Date _____ Date _____ Date _____

THURSDAY	FRIDAY	SATURDAY
8:00 am	8:00 am	
8:15 am	8:15 am	
8:30 am	8:30 am	
8:45 am	8:45 am	
9:00 am	9:00 am	
9:15 am	9:15 am	
9:30 am	9:30 am	
9:45 am	9:45 am	
10:00 am	10:00 am	
10:15 am	10:15 am	
10:30 am	10:30 am	
10:45 am	10:45 am	
11:00 am	11:00 am	
11:15 am	11:15 am	
11:30 am	11:30 am	
11:45 am	11:45 am	
12:00 pm	12:00 pm	
12:15 pm	12:15 pm	
12:30 pm	12:30 pm	
12:45 pm	12:45 pm	

THURSDAY	FRIDAY	SUNDAY
1:00 pm	1:00 pm	
1:15 pm	1:15 pm	
1:30 pm	1:30 pm	
1:45 pm	1:45 pm	
2:00 pm	2:00 pm	
2:15 pm	2:15 pm	
2:30 pm	2:30 pm	
2:45 pm	2:45 pm	
3:00 pm	3:00 pm	
3:15 pm	3:15 pm	
3:30 pm	3:30 pm	
3:45 pm	3:45 pm	
4:00 pm	4:00 pm	
4:15 pm	4:15 pm	
4:30 pm	4:30 pm	
4:45 pm	4:45 pm	
5:00 pm	5:00 pm	
5:15 pm	5:15 pm	
5:30 pm	5:30 pm	
5:45 pm	5:45 pm	
6:00 pm	6:00 pm	

TIME MANAGEMENT

PERSONAL DEVELOPMENT	INSPECT	JOB DESCRIPTION	CREATE MAGIC!

75

Date _____

MONDAY

8:00 am	
8:15 am	
8:30 am	
8:45 am	
9:00 am	
9:15 am	
9:30 am	
9:45 am	
10:00 am	
10:15 am	
10:30 am	
10:45 am	
11:00 am	
11:15 am	
11:30 am	
11:45 am	
12:00 pm	
12:15 pm	
12:30 pm	
12:45 pm	
1:00 pm	
1:15 pm	
1:30 pm	
1:45 pm	
2:00 pm	
2:15 pm	
2:30 pm	
2:45 pm	
3:00 pm	
3:15 pm	
3:30 pm	
3:45 pm	
4:00 pm	
4:15 pm	
4:30 pm	
4:45 pm	
5:00 pm	
5:15 pm	
5:30 pm	
5:45 pm	
6:00 pm	

Date _____

TUESDAY

8:00 am	
8:15 am	
8:30 am	
8:45 am	
9:00 am	
9:15 am	
9:30 am	
9:45 am	
10:00 am	
10:15 am	
10:30 am	
10:45 am	
11:00 am	
11:15 am	
11:30 am	
11:45 am	
12:00 pm	
12:15 pm	
12:30 pm	
12:45 pm	
1:00 pm	
1:15 pm	
1:30 pm	
1:45 pm	
2:00 pm	
2:15 pm	
2:30 pm	
2:45 pm	
3:00 pm	
3:15 pm	
3:30 pm	
3:45 pm	
4:00 pm	
4:15 pm	
4:30 pm	
4:45 pm	
5:00 pm	
5:15 pm	
5:30 pm	
5:45 pm	
6:00 pm	

Date _____

WEDNESDAY

8:00 am	
8:15 am	
8:30 am	
8:45 am	
9:00 am	
9:15 am	
9:30 am	
9:45 am	
10:00 am	
10:15 am	
10:30 am	
10:45 am	
11:00 am	
11:15 am	
11:30 am	
11:45 am	
12:00 pm	
12:15 pm	
12:30 pm	
12:45 pm	
1:00 pm	
1:15 pm	
1:30 pm	
1:45 pm	
2:00 pm	
2:15 pm	
2:30 pm	
2:45 pm	
3:00 pm	
3:15 pm	
3:30 pm	
3:45 pm	
4:00 pm	
4:15 pm	
4:30 pm	
4:45 pm	
5:00 pm	
5:15 pm	
5:30 pm	
5:45 pm	
6:00 pm	

TIME MANAGEMENT

PERSONAL DEVELOPMENT	INSPECT	JOB DESCRIPTION	CREATE MAGIC!

Date _____   Date _____   Date _____

THURSDAY	FRIDAY	SATURDAY
8:00 am	8:00 am	
8:15 am	8:15 am	
8:30 am	8:30 am	
8:45 am	8:45 am	
9:00 am	9:00 am	
9:15 am	9:15 am	
9:30 am	9:30 am	
9:45 am	9:45 am	
10:00 am	10:00 am	
10:15 am	10:15 am	
10:30 am	10:30 am	
10:45 am	10:45 am	
11:00 am	11:00 am	
11:15 am	11:15 am	
11:30 am	11:30 am	
11:45 am	11:45 am	
12:00 pm	12:00 pm	
12:15 pm	12:15 pm	
12:30 pm	12:30 pm	
12:45 pm	12:45 pm	

THURSDAY	FRIDAY	SUNDAY
1:00 pm	1:00 pm	
1:15 pm	1:15 pm	
1:30 pm	1:30 pm	
1:45 pm	1:45 pm	
2:00 pm	2:00 pm	
2:15 pm	2:15 pm	
2:30 pm	2:30 pm	
2:45 pm	2:45 pm	
3:00 pm	3:00 pm	
3:15 pm	3:15 pm	
3:30 pm	3:30 pm	
3:45 pm	3:45 pm	
4:00 pm	4:00 pm	
4:15 pm	4:15 pm	
4:30 pm	4:30 pm	
4:45 pm	4:45 pm	
5:00 pm	5:00 pm	
5:15 pm	5:15 pm	
5:30 pm	5:30 pm	
5:45 pm	5:45 pm	
6:00 pm	6:00 pm	

TIME MANAGEMENT

PERSONAL DEVELOPMENT	INSPECT	JOB DESCRIPTION	CREATE MAGIC!

77

Date _____   Date _____   Date _____

MONDAY	TUESDAY	WEDNESDAY
8:00 am	8:00 am	8:00 am
8:15 am	8:15 am	8:15 am
8:30 am	8:30 am	8:30 am
8:45 am	8:45 am	8:45 am
9:00 am	9:00 am	9:00 am
9:15 am	9:15 am	9:15 am
9:30 am	9:30 am	9:30 am
9:45 am	9:45 am	9:45 am
10:00 am	10:00 am	10:00 am
10:15 am	10:15 am	10:15 am
10:30 am	10:30 am	10:30 am
10:45 am	10:45 am	10:45 am
11:00 am	11:00 am	11:00 am
11:15 am	11:15 am	11:15 am
11:30 am	11:30 am	11:30 am
11:45 am	11:45 am	11:45 am
12:00 pm	12:00 pm	12:00 pm
12:15 pm	12:15 pm	12:15 pm
12:30 pm	12:30 pm	12:30 pm
12:45 pm	12:45 pm	12:45 pm
1:00 pm	1:00 pm	1:00 pm
1:15 pm	1:15 pm	1:15 pm
1:30 pm	1:30 pm	1:30 pm
1:45 pm	1:45 pm	1:45 pm
2:00 pm	2:00 pm	2:00 pm
2:15 pm	2:15 pm	2:15 pm
2:30 pm	2:30 pm	2:30 pm
2:45 pm	2:45 pm	2:45 pm
3:00 pm	3:00 pm	3:00 pm
3:15 pm	3:15 pm	3:15 pm
3:30 pm	3:30 pm	3:30 pm
3:45 pm	3:45 pm	3:45 pm
4:00 pm	4:00 pm	4:00 pm
4:15 pm	4:15 pm	4:15 pm
4:30 pm	4:30 pm	4:30 pm
4:45 pm	4:45 pm	4:45 pm
5:00 pm	5:00 pm	5:00 pm
5:15 pm	5:15 pm	5:15 pm
5:30 pm	5:30 pm	5:30 pm
5:45 pm	5:45 pm	5:45 pm
6:00 pm	6:00 pm	6:00 pm

TIME MANAGEMENT

PERSONAL DEVELOPMENT	INSPECT	JOB DESCRIPTION	CREATE MAGIC!

Date _____   Date _____   Date _____

THURSDAY		FRIDAY		SATURDAY

THURSDAY

8:00 am	
8:15 am	
8:30 am	
8:45 am	
9:00 am	
9:15 am	
9:30 am	
9:45 am	
10:00 am	
10:15 am	
10:30 am	
10:45 am	
11:00 am	
11:15 am	
11:30 am	
11:45 am	
12:00 pm	
12:15 pm	
12:30 pm	
12:45 pm	
1:00 pm	
1:15 pm	
1:30 pm	
1:45 pm	
2:00 pm	
2:15 pm	
2:30 pm	
2:45 pm	
3:00 pm	
3:15 pm	
3:30 pm	
3:45 pm	
4:00 pm	
4:15 pm	
4:30 pm	
4:45 pm	
5:00 pm	
5:15 pm	
5:30 pm	
5:45 pm	
6:00 pm	

FRIDAY

8:00 am	
8:15 am	
8:30 am	
8:45 am	
9:00 am	
9:15 am	
9:30 am	
9:45 am	
10:00 am	
10:15 am	
10:30 am	
10:45 am	
11:00 am	
11:15 am	
11:30 am	
11:45 am	
12:00 pm	
12:15 pm	
12:30 pm	
12:45 pm	
1:00 pm	
1:15 pm	
1:30 pm	
1:45 pm	
2:00 pm	
2:15 pm	
2:30 pm	
2:45 pm	
3:00 pm	
3:15 pm	
3:30 pm	
3:45 pm	
4:00 pm	
4:15 pm	
4:30 pm	
4:45 pm	
5:00 pm	
5:15 pm	
5:30 pm	
5:45 pm	
6:00 pm	

SATURDAY

SUNDAY

TIME MANAGEMENT

PERSONAL DEVELOPMENT	INSPECT	JOB DESCRIPTION	CREATE MAGIC!

Date _____ Date _____ Date _____

MONDAY	TUESDAY	WEDNESDAY
8:00 am	8:00 am	8:00 am
8:15 am	8:15 am	8:15 am
8:30 am	8:30 am	8:30 am
8:45 am	8:45 am	8:45 am
9:00 am	9:00 am	9:00 am
9:15 am	9:15 am	9:15 am
9:30 am	9:30 am	9:30 am
9:45 am	9:45 am	9:45 am
10:00 am	10:00 am	10:00 am
10:15 am	10:15 am	10:15 am
10:30 am	10:30 am	10:30 am
10:45 am	10:45 am	10:45 am
11:00 am	11:00 am	11:00 am
11:15 am	11:15 am	11:15 am
11:30 am	11:30 am	11:30 am
11:45 am	11:45 am	11:45 am
12:00 pm	12:00 pm	12:00 pm
12:15 pm	12:15 pm	12:15 pm
12:30 pm	12:30 pm	12:30 pm
12:45 pm	12:45 pm	12:45 pm
1:00 pm	1:00 pm	1:00 pm
1:15 pm	1:15 pm	1:15 pm
1:30 pm	1:30 pm	1:30 pm
1:45 pm	1:45 pm	1:45 pm
2:00 pm	2:00 pm	2:00 pm
2:15 pm	2:15 pm	2:15 pm
2:30 pm	2:30 pm	2:30 pm
2:45 pm	2:45 pm	2:45 pm
3:00 pm	3:00 pm	3:00 pm
3:15 pm	3:15 pm	3:15 pm
3:30 pm	3:30 pm	3:30 pm
3:45 pm	3:45 pm	3:45 pm
4:00 pm	4:00 pm	4:00 pm
4:15 pm	4:15 pm	4:15 pm
4:30 pm	4:30 pm	4:30 pm
4:45 pm	4:45 pm	4:45 pm
5:00 pm	5:00 pm	5:00 pm
5:15 pm	5:15 pm	5:15 pm
5:30 pm	5:30 pm	5:30 pm
5:45 pm	5:45 pm	5:45 pm
6:00 pm	6:00 pm	6:00 pm

TIME MANAGEMENT

PERSONAL DEVELOPMENT	INSPECT	JOB DESCRIPTION	CREATE MAGIC!

Date _____   Date _____   Date _____

THURSDAY		FRIDAY		SATURDAY	
8:00 am		8:00 am			
8:15 am		8:15 am			
8:30 am		8:30 am			
8:45 am		8:45 am			
9:00 am		9:00 am			
9:15 am		9:15 am			
9:30 am		9:30 am			
9:45 am		9:45 am			
10:00 am		10:00 am			
10:15 am		10:15 am			
10:30 am		10:30 am			
10:45 am		10:45 am			
11:00 am		11:00 am			
11:15 am		11:15 am			
11:30 am		11:30 am			
11:45 am		11:45 am			
12:00 pm		12:00 pm			
12:15 pm		12:15 pm			
12:30 pm		12:30 pm			
12:45 pm		12:45 pm			
1:00 pm		1:00 pm		SUNDAY	
1:15 pm		1:15 pm			
1:30 pm		1:30 pm			
1:45 pm		1:45 pm			
2:00 pm		2:00 pm			
2:15 pm		2:15 pm			
2:30 pm		2:30 pm			
2:45 pm		2:45 pm			
3:00 pm		3:00 pm			
3:15 pm		3:15 pm			
3:30 pm		3:30 pm			
3:45 pm		3:45 pm			
4:00 pm		4:00 pm			
4:15 pm		4:15 pm			
4:30 pm		4:30 pm			
4:45 pm		4:45 pm			
5:00 pm		5:00 pm			
5:15 pm		5:15 pm			
5:30 pm		5:30 pm			
5:45 pm		5:45 pm			
6:00 pm		6:00 pm			

TIME MANAGEMENT

PERSONAL DEVELOPMENT	INSPECT	JOB DESCRIPTION	CREATE MAGIC!

Date _____

MONDAY

8:00 am	
8:15 am	
8:30 am	
8:45 am	
9:00 am	
9:15 am	
9:30 am	
9:45 am	
10:00 am	
10:15 am	
10:30 am	
10:45 am	
11:00 am	
11:15 am	
11:30 am	
11:45 am	
12:00 pm	
12:15 pm	
12:30 pm	
12:45 pm	
1:00 pm	
1:15 pm	
1:30 pm	
1:45 pm	
2:00 pm	
2:15 pm	
2:30 pm	
2:45 pm	
3:00 pm	
3:15 pm	
3:30 pm	
3:45 pm	
4:00 pm	
4:15 pm	
4:30 pm	
4:45 pm	
5:00 pm	
5:15 pm	
5:30 pm	
5:45 pm	
6:00 pm	

Date _____

TUESDAY

8:00 am	
8:15 am	
8:30 am	
8:45 am	
9:00 am	
9:15 am	
9:30 am	
9:45 am	
10:00 am	
10:15 am	
10:30 am	
10:45 am	
11:00 am	
11:15 am	
11:30 am	
11:45 am	
12:00 pm	
12:15 pm	
12:30 pm	
12:45 pm	
1:00 pm	
1:15 pm	
1:30 pm	
1:45 pm	
2:00 pm	
2:15 pm	
2:30 pm	
2:45 pm	
3:00 pm	
3:15 pm	
3:30 pm	
3:45 pm	
4:00 pm	
4:15 pm	
4:30 pm	
4:45 pm	
5:00 pm	
5:15 pm	
5:30 pm	
5:45 pm	
6:00 pm	

Date _____

WEDNESDAY

8:00 am	
8:15 am	
8:30 am	
8:45 am	
9:00 am	
9:15 am	
9:30 am	
9:45 am	
10:00 am	
10:15 am	
10:30 am	
10:45 am	
11:00 am	
11:15 am	
11:30 am	
11:45 am	
12:00 pm	
12:15 pm	
12:30 pm	
12:45 pm	
1:00 pm	
1:15 pm	
1:30 pm	
1:45 pm	
2:00 pm	
2:15 pm	
2:30 pm	
2:45 pm	
3:00 pm	
3:15 pm	
3:30 pm	
3:45 pm	
4:00 pm	
4:15 pm	
4:30 pm	
4:45 pm	
5:00 pm	
5:15 pm	
5:30 pm	
5:45 pm	
6:00 pm	

TIME MANAGEMENT

PERSONAL DEVELOPMENT	INSPECT	JOB DESCRIPTION	CREATE MAGIC!

Date _____ Date _____ Date _____

THURSDAY	FRIDAY	SATURDAY
8:00 am	8:00 am	
8:15 am	8:15 am	
8:30 am	8:30 am	
8:45 am	8:45 am	
9:00 am	9:00 am	
9:15 am	9:15 am	
9:30 am	9:30 am	
9:45 am	9:45 am	
10:00 am	10:00 am	
10:15 am	10:15 am	
10:30 am	10:30 am	
10:45 am	10:45 am	
11:00 am	11:00 am	
11:15 am	11:15 am	
11:30 am	11:30 am	
11:45 am	11:45 am	
12:00 pm	12:00 pm	
12:15 pm	12:15 pm	
12:30 pm	12:30 pm	
12:45 pm	12:45 pm	
1:00 pm	1:00 pm	

		SUNDAY
1:15 pm	1:15 pm	
1:30 pm	1:30 pm	
1:45 pm	1:45 pm	
2:00 pm	2:00 pm	
2:15 pm	2:15 pm	
2:30 pm	2:30 pm	
2:45 pm	2:45 pm	
3:00 pm	3:00 pm	
3:15 pm	3:15 pm	
3:30 pm	3:30 pm	
3:45 pm	3:45 pm	
4:00 pm	4:00 pm	
4:15 pm	4:15 pm	
4:30 pm	4:30 pm	
4:45 pm	4:45 pm	
5:00 pm	5:00 pm	
5:15 pm	5:15 pm	
5:30 pm	5:30 pm	
5:45 pm	5:45 pm	
6:00 pm	6:00 pm	

TIME MANAGEMENT

PERSONAL DEVELOPMENT	INSPECT	JOB DESCRIPTION	CREATE MAGIC!

Date _____ Date _____ Date _____

MONDAY	TUESDAY	WEDNESDAY
8:00 am	8:00 am	8:00 am
8:15 am	8:15 am	8:15 am
8:30 am	8:30 am	8:30 am
8:45 am	8:45 am	8:45 am
9:00 am	9:00 am	9:00 am
9:15 am	9:15 am	9:15 am
9:30 am	9:30 am	9:30 am
9:45 am	9:45 am	9:45 am
10:00 am	10:00 am	10:00 am
10:15 am	10:15 am	10:15 am
10:30 am	10:30 am	10:30 am
10:45 am	10:45 am	10:45 am
11:00 am	11:00 am	11:00 am
11:15 am	11:15 am	11:15 am
11:30 am	11:30 am	11:30 am
11:45 am	11:45 am	11:45 am
12:00 pm	12:00 pm	12:00 pm
12:15 pm	12:15 pm	12:15 pm
12:30 pm	12:30 pm	12:30 pm
12:45 pm	12:45 pm	12:45 pm
1:00 pm	1:00 pm	1:00 pm
1:15 pm	1:15 pm	1:15 pm
1:30 pm	1:30 pm	1:30 pm
1:45 pm	1:45 pm	1:45 pm
2:00 pm	2:00 pm	2:00 pm
2:15 pm	2:15 pm	2:15 pm
2:30 pm	2:30 pm	2:30 pm
2:45 pm	2:45 pm	2:45 pm
3:00 pm	3:00 pm	3:00 pm
3:15 pm	3:15 pm	3:15 pm
3:30 pm	3:30 pm	3:30 pm
3:45 pm	3:45 pm	3:45 pm
4:00 pm	4:00 pm	4:00 pm
4:15 pm	4:15 pm	4:15 pm
4:30 pm	4:30 pm	4:30 pm
4:45 pm	4:45 pm	4:45 pm
5:00 pm	5:00 pm	5:00 pm
5:15 pm	5:15 pm	5:15 pm
5:30 pm	5:30 pm	5:30 pm
5:45 pm	5:45 pm	5:45 pm
6:00 pm	6:00 pm	6:00 pm

TIME MANAGEMENT

PERSONAL DEVELOPMENT	INSPECT	JOB DESCRIPTION	CREATE MAGIC!

Date _____   Date _____   Date _____

THURSDAY		FRIDAY		SATURDAY	
8:00 am		8:00 am			
8:15 am		8:15 am			
8:30 am		8:30 am			
8:45 am		8:45 am			
9:00 am		9:00 am			
9:15 am		9:15 am			
9:30 am		9:30 am			
9:45 am		9:45 am			
10:00 am		10:00 am			
10:15 am		10:15 am			
10:30 am		10:30 am			
10:45 am		10:45 am			
11:00 am		11:00 am			
11:15 am		11:15 am			
11:30 am		11:30 am			
11:45 am		11:45 am			
12:00 pm		12:00 pm			
12:15 pm		12:15 pm			
12:30 pm		12:30 pm			
12:45 pm		12:45 pm			

THURSDAY		FRIDAY		SUNDAY	
1:00 pm		1:00 pm			
1:15 pm		1:15 pm			
1:30 pm		1:30 pm			
1:45 pm		1:45 pm			
2:00 pm		2:00 pm			
2:15 pm		2:15 pm			
2:30 pm		2:30 pm			
2:45 pm		2:45 pm			
3:00 pm		3:00 pm			
3:15 pm		3:15 pm			
3:30 pm		3:30 pm			
3:45 pm		3:45 pm			
4:00 pm		4:00 pm			
4:15 pm		4:15 pm			
4:30 pm		4:30 pm			
4:45 pm		4:45 pm			
5:00 pm		5:00 pm			
5:15 pm		5:15 pm			
5:30 pm		5:30 pm			
5:45 pm		5:45 pm			
6:00 pm		6:00 pm			

TIME MANAGEMENT

PERSONAL DEVELOPMENT	INSPECT	JOB DESCRIPTION	CREATE MAGIC!

85

Date _____   Date _____   Date _____

MONDAY	TUESDAY	WEDNESDAY
8:00 am	8:00 am	8:00 am
8:15 am	8:15 am	8:15 am
8:30 am	8:30 am	8:30 am
8:45 am	8:45 am	8:45 am
9:00 am	9:00 am	9:00 am
9:15 am	9:15 am	9:15 am
9:30 am	9:30 am	9:30 am
9:45 am	9:45 am	9:45 am
10:00 am	10:00 am	10:00 am
10:15 am	10:15 am	10:15 am
10:30 am	10:30 am	10:30 am
10:45 am	10:45 am	10:45 am
11:00 am	11:00 am	11:00 am
11:15 am	11:15 am	11:15 am
11:30 am	11:30 am	11:30 am
11:45 am	11:45 am	11:45 am
12:00 pm	12:00 pm	12:00 pm
12:15 pm	12:15 pm	12:15 pm
12:30 pm	12:30 pm	12:30 pm
12:45 pm	12:45 pm	12:45 pm
1:00 pm	1:00 pm	1:00 pm
1:15 pm	1:15 pm	1:15 pm
1:30 pm	1:30 pm	1:30 pm
1:45 pm	1:45 pm	1:45 pm
2:00 pm	2:00 pm	2:00 pm
2:15 pm	2:15 pm	2:15 pm
2:30 pm	2:30 pm	2:30 pm
2:45 pm	2:45 pm	2:45 pm
3:00 pm	3:00 pm	3:00 pm
3:15 pm	3:15 pm	3:15 pm
3:30 pm	3:30 pm	3:30 pm
3:45 pm	3:45 pm	3:45 pm
4:00 pm	4:00 pm	4:00 pm
4:15 pm	4:15 pm	4:15 pm
4:30 pm	4:30 pm	4:30 pm
4:45 pm	4:45 pm	4:45 pm
5:00 pm	5:00 pm	5:00 pm
5:15 pm	5:15 pm	5:15 pm
5:30 pm	5:30 pm	5:30 pm
5:45 pm	5:45 pm	5:45 pm
6:00 pm	6:00 pm	6:00 pm

TIME MANAGEMENT

PERSONAL DEVELOPMENT	INSPECT	JOB DESCRIPTION	CREATE MAGIC!

Date _____ Date _____ Date _____

THURSDAY

8:00 am	
8:15 am	
8:30 am	
8:45 am	
9:00 am	
9:15 am	
9:30 am	
9:45 am	
10:00 am	
10:15 am	
10:30 am	
10:45 am	
11:00 am	
11:15 am	
11:30 am	
11:45 am	
12:00 pm	
12:15 pm	
12:30 pm	
12:45 pm	
1:00 pm	
1:15 pm	
1:30 pm	
1:45 pm	
2:00 pm	
2:15 pm	
2:30 pm	
2:45 pm	
3:00 pm	
3:15 pm	
3:30 pm	
3:45 pm	
4:00 pm	
4:15 pm	
4:30 pm	
4:45 pm	
5:00 pm	
5:15 pm	
5:30 pm	
5:45 pm	
6:00 pm	

FRIDAY

8:00 am	
8:15 am	
8:30 am	
8:45 am	
9:00 am	
9:15 am	
9:30 am	
9:45 am	
10:00 am	
10:15 am	
10:30 am	
10:45 am	
11:00 am	
11:15 am	
11:30 am	
11:45 am	
12:00 pm	
12:15 pm	
12:30 pm	
12:45 pm	
1:00 pm	
1:15 pm	
1:30 pm	
1:45 pm	
2:00 pm	
2:15 pm	
2:30 pm	
2:45 pm	
3:00 pm	
3:15 pm	
3:30 pm	
3:45 pm	
4:00 pm	
4:15 pm	
4:30 pm	
4:45 pm	
5:00 pm	
5:15 pm	
5:30 pm	
5:45 pm	
6:00 pm	

SATURDAY

SUNDAY

TIME MANAGEMENT

PERSONAL DEVELOPMENT	INSPECT	JOB DESCRIPTION	CREATE MAGIC!

87

Date _____   Date _____   Date _____

MONDAY	TUESDAY	WEDNESDAY
8:00 am	8:00 am	8:00 am
8:15 am	8:15 am	8:15 am
8:30 am	8:30 am	8:30 am
8:45 am	8:45 am	8:45 am
9:00 am	9:00 am	9:00 am
9:15 am	9:15 am	9:15 am
9:30 am	9:30 am	9:30 am
9:45 am	9:45 am	9:45 am
10:00 am	10:00 am	10:00 am
10:15 am	10:15 am	10:15 am
10:30 am	10:30 am	10:30 am
10:45 am	10:45 am	10:45 am
11:00 am	11:00 am	11:00 am
11:15 am	11:15 am	11:15 am
11:30 am	11:30 am	11:30 am
11:45 am	11:45 am	11:45 am
12:00 pm	12:00 pm	12:00 pm
12:15 pm	12:15 pm	12:15 pm
12:30 pm	12:30 pm	12:30 pm
12:45 pm	12:45 pm	12:45 pm
1:00 pm	1:00 pm	1:00 pm
1:15 pm	1:15 pm	1:15 pm
1:30 pm	1:30 pm	1:30 pm
1:45 pm	1:45 pm	1:45 pm
2:00 pm	2:00 pm	2:00 pm
2:15 pm	2:15 pm	2:15 pm
2:30 pm	2:30 pm	2:30 pm
2:45 pm	2:45 pm	2:45 pm
3:00 pm	3:00 pm	3:00 pm
3:15 pm	3:15 pm	3:15 pm
3:30 pm	3:30 pm	3:30 pm
3:45 pm	3:45 pm	3:45 pm
4:00 pm	4:00 pm	4:00 pm
4:15 pm	4:15 pm	4:15 pm
4:30 pm	4:30 pm	4:30 pm
4:45 pm	4:45 pm	4:45 pm
5:00 pm	5:00 pm	5:00 pm
5:15 pm	5:15 pm	5:15 pm
5:30 pm	5:30 pm	5:30 pm
5:45 pm	5:45 pm	5:45 pm
6:00 pm	6:00 pm	6:00 pm

TIME MANAGEMENT

PERSONAL DEVELOPMENT	INSPECT	JOB DESCRIPTION	CREATE MAGIC!

Date _____   Date _____   Date _____

THURSDAY	FRIDAY	SATURDAY

THURSDAY		FRIDAY		SATURDAY	
8:00 am		8:00 am			
8:15 am		8:15 am			
8:30 am		8:30 am			
8:45 am		8:45 am			
9:00 am		9:00 am			
9:15 am		9:15 am			
9:30 am		9:30 am			
9:45 am		9:45 am			
10:00 am		10:00 am			
10:15 am		10:15 am			
10:30 am		10:30 am			
10:45 am		10:45 am			
11:00 am		11:00 am			
11:15 am		11:15 am			
11:30 am		11:30 am			
11:45 am		11:45 am			
12:00 pm		12:00 pm			
12:15 pm		12:15 pm			
12:30 pm		12:30 pm			
12:45 pm		12:45 pm			
1:00 pm		1:00 pm		SUNDAY	
1:15 pm		1:15 pm			
1:30 pm		1:30 pm			
1:45 pm		1:45 pm			
2:00 pm		2:00 pm			
2:15 pm		2:15 pm			
2:30 pm		2:30 pm			
2:45 pm		2:45 pm			
3:00 pm		3:00 pm			
3:15 pm		3:15 pm			
3:30 pm		3:30 pm			
3:45 pm		3:45 pm			
4:00 pm		4:00 pm			
4:15 pm		4:15 pm			
4:30 pm		4:30 pm			
4:45 pm		4:45 pm			
5:00 pm		5:00 pm			
5:15 pm		5:15 pm			
5:30 pm		5:30 pm			
5:45 pm		5:45 pm			
6:00 pm		6:00 pm			

TIME MANAGEMENT

PERSONAL DEVELOPMENT	INSPECT	JOB DESCRIPTION	CREATE MAGIC!

Date _____

MONDAY

8:00 am	
8:15 am	
8:30 am	
8:45 am	
9:00 am	
9:15 am	
9:30 am	
9:45 am	
10:00 am	
10:15 am	
10:30 am	
10:45 am	
11:00 am	
11:15 am	
11:30 am	
11:45 am	
12:00 pm	
12:15 pm	
12:30 pm	
12:45 pm	
1:00 pm	
1:15 pm	
1:30 pm	
1:45 pm	
2:00 pm	
2:15 pm	
2:30 pm	
2:45 pm	
3:00 pm	
3:15 pm	
3:30 pm	
3:45 pm	
4:00 pm	
4:15 pm	
4:30 pm	
4:45 pm	
5:00 pm	
5:15 pm	
5:30 pm	
5:45 pm	
6:00 pm	

Date _____

TUESDAY

8:00 am	
8:15 am	
8:30 am	
8:45 am	
9:00 am	
9:15 am	
9:30 am	
9:45 am	
10:00 am	
10:15 am	
10:30 am	
10:45 am	
11:00 am	
11:15 am	
11:30 am	
11:45 am	
12:00 pm	
12:15 pm	
12:30 pm	
12:45 pm	
1:00 pm	
1:15 pm	
1:30 pm	
1:45 pm	
2:00 pm	
2:15 pm	
2:30 pm	
2:45 pm	
3:00 pm	
3:15 pm	
3:30 pm	
3:45 pm	
4:00 pm	
4:15 pm	
4:30 pm	
4:45 pm	
5:00 pm	
5:15 pm	
5:30 pm	
5:45 pm	
6:00 pm	

Date _____

WEDNESDAY

8:00 am	
8:15 am	
8:30 am	
8:45 am	
9:00 am	
9:15 am	
9:30 am	
9:45 am	
10:00 am	
10:15 am	
10:30 am	
10:45 am	
11:00 am	
11:15 am	
11:30 am	
11:45 am	
12:00 pm	
12:15 pm	
12:30 pm	
12:45 pm	
1:00 pm	
1:15 pm	
1:30 pm	
1:45 pm	
2:00 pm	
2:15 pm	
2:30 pm	
2:45 pm	
3:00 pm	
3:15 pm	
3:30 pm	
3:45 pm	
4:00 pm	
4:15 pm	
4:30 pm	
4:45 pm	
5:00 pm	
5:15 pm	
5:30 pm	
5:45 pm	
6:00 pm	

TIME MANAGEMENT

PERSONAL DEVELOPMENT	INSPECT	JOB DESCRIPTION	CREATE MAGIC!

Date _____   Date _____   Date _____

THURSDAY	FRIDAY	SATURDAY

THURSDAY		FRIDAY		SATURDAY
8:00 am		8:00 am		
8:15 am		8:15 am		
8:30 am		8:30 am		
8:45 am		8:45 am		
9:00 am		9:00 am		
9:15 am		9:15 am		
9:30 am		9:30 am		
9:45 am		9:45 am		
10:00 am		10:00 am		
10:15 am		10:15 am		
10:30 am		10:30 am		
10:45 am		10:45 am		
11:00 am		11:00 am		
11:15 am		11:15 am		
11:30 am		11:30 am		
11:45 am		11:45 am		
12:00 pm		12:00 pm		
12:15 pm		12:15 pm		
12:30 pm		12:30 pm		
12:45 pm		12:45 pm		
1:00 pm		1:00 pm		SUNDAY
1:15 pm		1:15 pm		
1:30 pm		1:30 pm		
1:45 pm		1:45 pm		
2:00 pm		2:00 pm		
2:15 pm		2:15 pm		
2:30 pm		2:30 pm		
2:45 pm		2:45 pm		
3:00 pm		3:00 pm		
3:15 pm		3:15 pm		
3:30 pm		3:30 pm		
3:45 pm		3:45 pm		
4:00 pm		4:00 pm		
4:15 pm		4:15 pm		
4:30 pm		4:30 pm		
4:45 pm		4:45 pm		
5:00 pm		5:00 pm		
5:15 pm		5:15 pm		
5:30 pm		5:30 pm		
5:45 pm		5:45 pm		
6:00 pm		6:00 pm		

DAILY PLANNER

SUNDAY

TIME MANAGEMENT

PERSONAL DEVELOPMENT	INSPECT	JOB DESCRIPTION	CREATE MAGIC!

Date _____

MONDAY

8:00 am	
8:15 am	
8:30 am	
8:45 am	
9:00 am	
9:15 am	
9:30 am	
9:45 am	
10:00 am	
10:15 am	
10:30 am	
10:45 am	
11:00 am	
11:15 am	
11:30 am	
11:45 am	
12:00 pm	
12:15 pm	
12:30 pm	
12:45 pm	
1:00 pm	
1:15 pm	
1:30 pm	
1:45 pm	
2:00 pm	
2:15 pm	
2:30 pm	
2:45 pm	
3:00 pm	
3:15 pm	
3:30 pm	
3:45 pm	
4:00 pm	
4:15 pm	
4:30 pm	
4:45 pm	
5:00 pm	
5:15 pm	
5:30 pm	
5:45 pm	
6:00 pm	

Date _____

TUESDAY

8:00 am	
8:15 am	
8:30 am	
8:45 am	
9:00 am	
9:15 am	
9:30 am	
9:45 am	
10:00 am	
10:15 am	
10:30 am	
10:45 am	
11:00 am	
11:15 am	
11:30 am	
11:45 am	
12:00 pm	
12:15 pm	
12:30 pm	
12:45 pm	
1:00 pm	
1:15 pm	
1:30 pm	
1:45 pm	
2:00 pm	
2:15 pm	
2:30 pm	
2:45 pm	
3:00 pm	
3:15 pm	
3:30 pm	
3:45 pm	
4:00 pm	
4:15 pm	
4:30 pm	
4:45 pm	
5:00 pm	
5:15 pm	
5:30 pm	
5:45 pm	
6:00 pm	

Date _____

WEDNESDAY

8:00 am	
8:15 am	
8:30 am	
8:45 am	
9:00 am	
9:15 am	
9:30 am	
9:45 am	
10:00 am	
10:15 am	
10:30 am	
10:45 am	
11:00 am	
11:15 am	
11:30 am	
11:45 am	
12:00 pm	
12:15 pm	
12:30 pm	
12:45 pm	
1:00 pm	
1:15 pm	
1:30 pm	
1:45 pm	
2:00 pm	
2:15 pm	
2:30 pm	
2:45 pm	
3:00 pm	
3:15 pm	
3:30 pm	
3:45 pm	
4:00 pm	
4:15 pm	
4:30 pm	
4:45 pm	
5:00 pm	
5:15 pm	
5:30 pm	
5:45 pm	
6:00 pm	

TIME MANAGEMENT

PERSONAL DEVELOPMENT	INSPECT	JOB DESCRIPTION	CREATE MAGIC!

Date _____

THURSDAY

8:00 am	
8:15 am	
8:30 am	
8:45 am	
9:00 am	
9:15 am	
9:30 am	
9:45 am	
10:00 am	
10:15 am	
10:30 am	
10:45 am	
11:00 am	
11:15 am	
11:30 am	
11:45 am	
12:00 pm	
12:15 pm	
12:30 pm	
12:45 pm	
1:00 pm	
1:15 pm	
1:30 pm	
1:45 pm	
2:00 pm	
2:15 pm	
2:30 pm	
2:45 pm	
3:00 pm	
3:15 pm	
3:30 pm	
3:45 pm	
4:00 pm	
4:15 pm	
4:30 pm	
4:45 pm	
5:00 pm	
5:15 pm	
5:30 pm	
5:45 pm	
6:00 pm	

Date _____

FRIDAY

8:00 am	
8:15 am	
8:30 am	
8:45 am	
9:00 am	
9:15 am	
9:30 am	
9:45 am	
10:00 am	
10:15 am	
10:30 am	
10:45 am	
11:00 am	
11:15 am	
11:30 am	
11:45 am	
12:00 pm	
12:15 pm	
12:30 pm	
12:45 pm	
1:00 pm	
1:15 pm	
1:30 pm	
1:45 pm	
2:00 pm	
2:15 pm	
2:30 pm	
2:45 pm	
3:00 pm	
3:15 pm	
3:30 pm	
3:45 pm	
4:00 pm	
4:15 pm	
4:30 pm	
4:45 pm	
5:00 pm	
5:15 pm	
5:30 pm	
5:45 pm	
6:00 pm	

Date _____

SATURDAY

SUNDAY

TIME MANAGEMENT

PERSONAL DEVELOPMENT	INSPECT	JOB DESCRIPTION	CREATE MAGIC!

93

Date _____

MONDAY

8:00 am	
8:15 am	
8:30 am	
8:45 am	
9:00 am	
9:15 am	
9:30 am	
9:45 am	
10:00 am	
10:15 am	
10:30 am	
10:45 am	
11:00 am	
11:15 am	
11:30 am	
11:45 am	
12:00 pm	
12:15 pm	
12:30 pm	
12:45 pm	
1:00 pm	
1:15 pm	
1:30 pm	
1:45 pm	
2:00 pm	
2:15 pm	
2:30 pm	
2:45 pm	
3:00 pm	
3:15 pm	
3:30 pm	
3:45 pm	
4:00 pm	
4:15 pm	
4:30 pm	
4:45 pm	
5:00 pm	
5:15 pm	
5:30 pm	
5:45 pm	
6:00 pm	

Date _____

TUESDAY

8:00 am	
8:15 am	
8:30 am	
8:45 am	
9:00 am	
9:15 am	
9:30 am	
9:45 am	
10:00 am	
10:15 am	
10:30 am	
10:45 am	
11:00 am	
11:15 am	
11:30 am	
11:45 am	
12:00 pm	
12:15 pm	
12:30 pm	
12:45 pm	
1:00 pm	
1:15 pm	
1:30 pm	
1:45 pm	
2:00 pm	
2:15 pm	
2:30 pm	
2:45 pm	
3:00 pm	
3:15 pm	
3:30 pm	
3:45 pm	
4:00 pm	
4:15 pm	
4:30 pm	
4:45 pm	
5:00 pm	
5:15 pm	
5:30 pm	
5:45 pm	
6:00 pm	

Date _____

WEDNESDAY

8:00 am	
8:15 am	
8:30 am	
8:45 am	
9:00 am	
9:15 am	
9:30 am	
9:45 am	
10:00 am	
10:15 am	
10:30 am	
10:45 am	
11:00 am	
11:15 am	
11:30 am	
11:45 am	
12:00 pm	
12:15 pm	
12:30 pm	
12:45 pm	
1:00 pm	
1:15 pm	
1:30 pm	
1:45 pm	
2:00 pm	
2:15 pm	
2:30 pm	
2:45 pm	
3:00 pm	
3:15 pm	
3:30 pm	
3:45 pm	
4:00 pm	
4:15 pm	
4:30 pm	
4:45 pm	
5:00 pm	
5:15 pm	
5:30 pm	
5:45 pm	
6:00 pm	

TIME MANAGEMENT

PERSONAL DEVELOPMENT	INSPECT	JOB DESCRIPTION	CREATE MAGIC!

Date _____   Date _____   Date _____

THURSDAY	FRIDAY	SATURDAY
8:00 am	8:00 am	
8:15 am	8:15 am	
8:30 am	8:30 am	
8:45 am	8:45 am	
9:00 am	9:00 am	
9:15 am	9:15 am	
9:30 am	9:30 am	
9:45 am	9:45 am	
10:00 am	10:00 am	
10:15 am	10:15 am	
10:30 am	10:30 am	
10:45 am	10:45 am	
11:00 am	11:00 am	
11:15 am	11:15 am	
11:30 am	11:30 am	
11:45 am	11:45 am	
12:00 pm	12:00 pm	
12:15 pm	12:15 pm	
12:30 pm	12:30 pm	
12:45 pm	12:45 pm	
1:00 pm	1:00 pm	**SUNDAY**
1:15 pm	1:15 pm	
1:30 pm	1:30 pm	
1:45 pm	1:45 pm	
2:00 pm	2:00 pm	
2:15 pm	2:15 pm	
2:30 pm	2:30 pm	
2:45 pm	2:45 pm	
3:00 pm	3:00 pm	
3:15 pm	3:15 pm	
3:30 pm	3:30 pm	
3:45 pm	3:45 pm	
4:00 pm	4:00 pm	
4:15 pm	4:15 pm	
4:30 pm	4:30 pm	
4:45 pm	4:45 pm	
5:00 pm	5:00 pm	
5:15 pm	5:15 pm	
5:30 pm	5:30 pm	
5:45 pm	5:45 pm	
6:00 pm	6:00 pm	

TIME MANAGEMENT

PERSONAL DEVELOPMENT	INSPECT	JOB DESCRIPTION	CREATE MAGIC!

Date _____

Date _____

Date _____

MONDAY	TUESDAY	WEDNESDAY
8:00 am	8:00 am	8:00 am
8:15 am	8:15 am	8:15 am
8:30 am	8:30 am	8:30 am
8:45 am	8:45 am	8:45 am
9:00 am	9:00 am	9:00 am
9:15 am	9:15 am	9:15 am
9:30 am	9:30 am	9:30 am
9:45 am	9:45 am	9:45 am
10:00 am	10:00 am	10:00 am
10:15 am	10:15 am	10:15 am
10:30 am	10:30 am	10:30 am
10:45 am	10:45 am	10:45 am
11:00 am	11:00 am	11:00 am
11:15 am	11:15 am	11:15 am
11:30 am	11:30 am	11:30 am
11:45 am	11:45 am	11:45 am
12:00 pm	12:00 pm	12:00 pm
12:15 pm	12:15 pm	12:15 pm
12:30 pm	12:30 pm	12:30 pm
12:45 pm	12:45 pm	12:45 pm
1:00 pm	1:00 pm	1:00 pm
1:15 pm	1:15 pm	1:15 pm
1:30 pm	1:30 pm	1:30 pm
1:45 pm	1:45 pm	1:45 pm
2:00 pm	2:00 pm	2:00 pm
2:15 pm	2:15 pm	2:15 pm
2:30 pm	2:30 pm	2:30 pm
2:45 pm	2:45 pm	2:45 pm
3:00 pm	3:00 pm	3:00 pm
3:15 pm	3:15 pm	3:15 pm
3:30 pm	3:30 pm	3:30 pm
3:45 pm	3:45 pm	3:45 pm
4:00 pm	4:00 pm	4:00 pm
4:15 pm	4:15 pm	4:15 pm
4:30 pm	4:30 pm	4:30 pm
4:45 pm	4:45 pm	4:45 pm
5:00 pm	5:00 pm	5:00 pm
5:15 pm	5:15 pm	5:15 pm
5:30 pm	5:30 pm	5:30 pm
5:45 pm	5:45 pm	5:45 pm
6:00 pm	6:00 pm	6:00 pm

TIME MANAGEMENT

PERSONAL DEVELOPMENT	INSPECT	JOB DESCRIPTION	CREATE MAGIC!

Date _____   Date _____   Date _____

THURSDAY		FRIDAY		SATURDAY	
8:00 am		8:00 am			
8:15 am		8:15 am			
8:30 am		8:30 am			
8:45 am		8:45 am			
9:00 am		9:00 am			
9:15 am		9:15 am			
9:30 am		9:30 am			
9:45 am		9:45 am			
10:00 am		10:00 am			
10:15 am		10:15 am			
10:30 am		10:30 am			
10:45 am		10:45 am			
11:00 am		11:00 am			
11:15 am		11:15 am			
11:30 am		11:30 am			
11:45 am		11:45 am			
12:00 pm		12:00 pm			
12:15 pm		12:15 pm			
12:30 pm		12:30 pm			
12:45 pm		12:45 pm			

				SUNDAY	
1:00 pm		1:00 pm			
1:15 pm		1:15 pm			
1:30 pm		1:30 pm			
1:45 pm		1:45 pm			
2:00 pm		2:00 pm			
2:15 pm		2:15 pm			
2:30 pm		2:30 pm			
2:45 pm		2:45 pm			
3:00 pm		3:00 pm			
3:15 pm		3:15 pm			
3:30 pm		3:30 pm			
3:45 pm		3:45 pm			
4:00 pm		4:00 pm			
4:15 pm		4:15 pm			
4:30 pm		4:30 pm			
4:45 pm		4:45 pm			
5:00 pm		5:00 pm			
5:15 pm		5:15 pm			
5:30 pm		5:30 pm			
5:45 pm		5:45 pm			
6:00 pm		6:00 pm			

TIME MANAGEMENT

PERSONAL DEVELOPMENT	INSPECT	JOB DESCRIPTION	CREATE MAGIC!

97

Date _____

MONDAY

8:00 am	
8:15 am	
8:30 am	
8:45 am	
9:00 am	
9:15 am	
9:30 am	
9:45 am	
10:00 am	
10:15 am	
10:30 am	
10:45 am	
11:00 am	
11:15 am	
11:30 am	
11:45 am	
12:00 pm	
12:15 pm	
12:30 pm	
12:45 pm	
1:00 pm	
1:15 pm	
1:30 pm	
1:45 pm	
2:00 pm	
2:15 pm	
2:30 pm	
2:45 pm	
3:00 pm	
3:15 pm	
3:30 pm	
3:45 pm	
4:00 pm	
4:15 pm	
4:30 pm	
4:45 pm	
5:00 pm	
5:15 pm	
5:30 pm	
5:45 pm	
6:00 pm	

Date _____

TUESDAY

8:00 am	
8:15 am	
8:30 am	
8:45 am	
9:00 am	
9:15 am	
9:30 am	
9:45 am	
10:00 am	
10:15 am	
10:30 am	
10:45 am	
11:00 am	
11:15 am	
11:30 am	
11:45 am	
12:00 pm	
12:15 pm	
12:30 pm	
12:45 pm	
1:00 pm	
1:15 pm	
1:30 pm	
1:45 pm	
2:00 pm	
2:15 pm	
2:30 pm	
2:45 pm	
3:00 pm	
3:15 pm	
3:30 pm	
3:45 pm	
4:00 pm	
4:15 pm	
4:30 pm	
4:45 pm	
5:00 pm	
5:15 pm	
5:30 pm	
5:45 pm	
6:00 pm	

Date _____

WEDNESDAY

8:00 am	
8:15 am	
8:30 am	
8:45 am	
9:00 am	
9:15 am	
9:30 am	
9:45 am	
10:00 am	
10:15 am	
10:30 am	
10:45 am	
11:00 am	
11:15 am	
11:30 am	
11:45 am	
12:00 pm	
12:15 pm	
12:30 pm	
12:45 pm	
1:00 pm	
1:15 pm	
1:30 pm	
1:45 pm	
2:00 pm	
2:15 pm	
2:30 pm	
2:45 pm	
3:00 pm	
3:15 pm	
3:30 pm	
3:45 pm	
4:00 pm	
4:15 pm	
4:30 pm	
4:45 pm	
5:00 pm	
5:15 pm	
5:30 pm	
5:45 pm	
6:00 pm	

TIME MANAGEMENT

PERSONAL DEVELOPMENT	INSPECT	JOB DESCRIPTION	CREATE MAGIC!

Date _____   Date _____   Date _____

THURSDAY		FRIDAY		SATURDAY	
8:00 am		8:00 am			
8:15 am		8:15 am			
8:30 am		8:30 am			
8:45 am		8:45 am			
9:00 am		9:00 am			
9:15 am		9:15 am			
9:30 am		9:30 am			
9:45 am		9:45 am			
10:00 am		10:00 am			
10:15 am		10:15 am			
10:30 am		10:30 am			
10:45 am		10:45 am			
11:00 am		11:00 am			
11:15 am		11:15 am			
11:30 am		11:30 am			
11:45 am		11:45 am			
12:00 pm		12:00 pm			
12:15 pm		12:15 pm			
12:30 pm		12:30 pm			
12:45 pm		12:45 pm			
1:00 pm		1:00 pm		SUNDAY	
1:15 pm		1:15 pm			
1:30 pm		1:30 pm			
1:45 pm		1:45 pm			
2:00 pm		2:00 pm			
2:15 pm		2:15 pm			
2:30 pm		2:30 pm			
2:45 pm		2:45 pm			
3:00 pm		3:00 pm			
3:15 pm		3:15 pm			
3:30 pm		3:30 pm			
3:45 pm		3:45 pm			
4:00 pm		4:00 pm			
4:15 pm		4:15 pm			
4:30 pm		4:30 pm			
4:45 pm		4:45 pm			
5:00 pm		5:00 pm			
5:15 pm		5:15 pm			
5:30 pm		5:30 pm			
5:45 pm		5:45 pm			
6:00 pm		6:00 pm			

TIME MANAGEMENT

PERSONAL DEVELOPMENT	INSPECT	JOB DESCRIPTION	CREATE MAGIC!

Date _____

MONDAY

8:00 am	
8:15 am	
8:30 am	
8:45 am	
9:00 am	
9:15 am	
9:30 am	
9:45 am	
10:00 am	
10:15 am	
10:30 am	
10:45 am	
11:00 am	
11:15 am	
11:30 am	
11:45 am	
12:00 pm	
12:15 pm	
12:30 pm	
12:45 pm	
1:00 pm	
1:15 pm	
1:30 pm	
1:45 pm	
2:00 pm	
2:15 pm	
2:30 pm	
2:45 pm	
3:00 pm	
3:15 pm	
3:30 pm	
3:45 pm	
4:00 pm	
4:15 pm	
4:30 pm	
4:45 pm	
5:00 pm	
5:15 pm	
5:30 pm	
5:45 pm	
6:00 pm	

Date _____

TUESDAY

8:00 am	
8:15 am	
8:30 am	
8:45 am	
9:00 am	
9:15 am	
9:30 am	
9:45 am	
10:00 am	
10:15 am	
10:30 am	
10:45 am	
11:00 am	
11:15 am	
11:30 am	
11:45 am	
12:00 pm	
12:15 pm	
12:30 pm	
12:45 pm	
1:00 pm	
1:15 pm	
1:30 pm	
1:45 pm	
2:00 pm	
2:15 pm	
2:30 pm	
2:45 pm	
3:00 pm	
3:15 pm	
3:30 pm	
3:45 pm	
4:00 pm	
4:15 pm	
4:30 pm	
4:45 pm	
5:00 pm	
5:15 pm	
5:30 pm	
5:45 pm	
6:00 pm	

Date _____

WEDNESDAY

8:00 am	
8:15 am	
8:30 am	
8:45 am	
9:00 am	
9:15 am	
9:30 am	
9:45 am	
10:00 am	
10:15 am	
10:30 am	
10:45 am	
11:00 am	
11:15 am	
11:30 am	
11:45 am	
12:00 pm	
12:15 pm	
12:30 pm	
12:45 pm	
1:00 pm	
1:15 pm	
1:30 pm	
1:45 pm	
2:00 pm	
2:15 pm	
2:30 pm	
2:45 pm	
3:00 pm	
3:15 pm	
3:30 pm	
3:45 pm	
4:00 pm	
4:15 pm	
4:30 pm	
4:45 pm	
5:00 pm	
5:15 pm	
5:30 pm	
5:45 pm	
6:00 pm	

TIME MANAGEMENT

PERSONAL DEVELOPMENT	INSPECT	JOB DESCRIPTION	CREATE MAGIC!

Date _____ Date _____ Date _____

THURSDAY	FRIDAY	SATURDAY

THURSDAY	FRIDAY
8:00 am	8:00 am
8:15 am	8:15 am
8:30 am	8:30 am
8:45 am	8:45 am
9:00 am	9:00 am
9:15 am	9:15 am
9:30 am	9:30 am
9:45 am	9:45 am
10:00 am	10:00 am
10:15 am	10:15 am
10:30 am	10:30 am
10:45 am	10:45 am
11:00 am	11:00 am
11:15 am	11:15 am
11:30 am	11:30 am
11:45 am	11:45 am
12:00 pm	12:00 pm
12:15 pm	12:15 pm
12:30 pm	12:30 pm
12:45 pm	12:45 pm
1:00 pm	1:00 pm
1:15 pm	1:15 pm
1:30 pm	1:30 pm
1:45 pm	1:45 pm
2:00 pm	2:00 pm
2:15 pm	2:15 pm
2:30 pm	2:30 pm
2:45 pm	2:45 pm
3:00 pm	3:00 pm
3:15 pm	3:15 pm
3:30 pm	3:30 pm
3:45 pm	3:45 pm
4:00 pm	4:00 pm
4:15 pm	4:15 pm
4:30 pm	4:30 pm
4:45 pm	4:45 pm
5:00 pm	5:00 pm
5:15 pm	5:15 pm
5:30 pm	5:30 pm
5:45 pm	5:45 pm
6:00 pm	6:00 pm

SUNDAY

TIME MANAGEMENT

PERSONAL DEVELOPMENT	INSPECT	JOB DESCRIPTION	CREATE MAGIC!

101

Date _____

MONDAY

8:00 am	
8:15 am	
8:30 am	
8:45 am	
9:00 am	
9:15 am	
9:30 am	
9:45 am	
10:00 am	
10:15 am	
10:30 am	
10:45 am	
11:00 am	
11:15 am	
11:30 am	
11:45 am	
12:00 pm	
12:15 pm	
12:30 pm	
12:45 pm	
1:00 pm	
1:15 pm	
1:30 pm	
1:45 pm	
2:00 pm	
2:15 pm	
2:30 pm	
2:45 pm	
3:00 pm	
3:15 pm	
3:30 pm	
3:45 pm	
4:00 pm	
4:15 pm	
4:30 pm	
4:45 pm	
5:00 pm	
5:15 pm	
5:30 pm	
5:45 pm	
6:00 pm	

Date _____

TUESDAY

8:00 am	
8:15 am	
8:30 am	
8:45 am	
9:00 am	
9:15 am	
9:30 am	
9:45 am	
10:00 am	
10:15 am	
10:30 am	
10:45 am	
11:00 am	
11:15 am	
11:30 am	
11:45 am	
12:00 pm	
12:15 pm	
12:30 pm	
12:45 pm	
1:00 pm	
1:15 pm	
1:30 pm	
1:45 pm	
2:00 pm	
2:15 pm	
2:30 pm	
2:45 pm	
3:00 pm	
3:15 pm	
3:30 pm	
3:45 pm	
4:00 pm	
4:15 pm	
4:30 pm	
4:45 pm	
5:00 pm	
5:15 pm	
5:30 pm	
5:45 pm	
6:00 pm	

Date _____

WEDNESDAY

8:00 am	
8:15 am	
8:30 am	
8:45 am	
9:00 am	
9:15 am	
9:30 am	
9:45 am	
10:00 am	
10:15 am	
10:30 am	
10:45 am	
11:00 am	
11:15 am	
11:30 am	
11:45 am	
12:00 pm	
12:15 pm	
12:30 pm	
12:45 pm	
1:00 pm	
1:15 pm	
1:30 pm	
1:45 pm	
2:00 pm	
2:15 pm	
2:30 pm	
2:45 pm	
3:00 pm	
3:15 pm	
3:30 pm	
3:45 pm	
4:00 pm	
4:15 pm	
4:30 pm	
4:45 pm	
5:00 pm	
5:15 pm	
5:30 pm	
5:45 pm	
6:00 pm	

DAILY PLANNER

TIME MANAGEMENT

PERSONAL DEVELOPMENT	INSPECT	JOB DESCRIPTION	CREATE MAGIC!

102

Date _____   Date _____   Date _____

THURSDAY	FRIDAY	SATURDAY

DAILY PLANNER

THURSDAY

8:00 am
8:15 am
8:30 am
8:45 am
9:00 am
9:15 am
9:30 am
9:45 am
10:00 am
10:15 am
10:30 am
10:45 am
11:00 am
11:15 am
11:30 am
11:45 am
12:00 pm
12:15 pm
12:30 pm
12:45 pm
1:00 pm
1:15 pm
1:30 pm
1:45 pm
2:00 pm
2:15 pm
2:30 pm
2:45 pm
3:00 pm
3:15 pm
3:30 pm
3:45 pm
4:00 pm
4:15 pm
4:30 pm
4:45 pm
5:00 pm
5:15 pm
5:30 pm
5:45 pm
6:00 pm

FRIDAY

8:00 am
8:15 am
8:30 am
8:45 am
9:00 am
9:15 am
9:30 am
9:45 am
10:00 am
10:15 am
10:30 am
10:45 am
11:00 am
11:15 am
11:30 am
11:45 am
12:00 pm
12:15 pm
12:30 pm
12:45 pm
1:00 pm
1:15 pm
1:30 pm
1:45 pm
2:00 pm
2:15 pm
2:30 pm
2:45 pm
3:00 pm
3:15 pm
3:30 pm
3:45 pm
4:00 pm
4:15 pm
4:30 pm
4:45 pm
5:00 pm
5:15 pm
5:30 pm
5:45 pm
6:00 pm

SATURDAY

SUNDAY

TIME MANAGEMENT

PERSONAL DEVELOPMENT	INSPECT	JOB DESCRIPTION	CREATE MAGIC!

Date _____ Date _____ Date _____

MONDAY	TUESDAY	WEDNESDAY
8:00 am	8:00 am	8:00 am
8:15 am	8:15 am	8:15 am
8:30 am	8:30 am	8:30 am
8:45 am	8:45 am	8:45 am
9:00 am	9:00 am	9:00 am
9:15 am	9:15 am	9:15 am
9:30 am	9:30 am	9:30 am
9:45 am	9:45 am	9:45 am
10:00 am	10:00 am	10:00 am
10:15 am	10:15 am	10:15 am
10:30 am	10:30 am	10:30 am
10:45 am	10:45 am	10:45 am
11:00 am	11:00 am	11:00 am
11:15 am	11:15 am	11:15 am
11:30 am	11:30 am	11:30 am
11:45 am	11:45 am	11:45 am
12:00 pm	12:00 pm	12:00 pm
12:15 pm	12:15 pm	12:15 pm
12:30 pm	12:30 pm	12:30 pm
12:45 pm	12:45 pm	12:45 pm
1:00 pm	1:00 pm	1:00 pm
1:15 pm	1:15 pm	1:15 pm
1:30 pm	1:30 pm	1:30 pm
1:45 pm	1:45 pm	1:45 pm
2:00 pm	2:00 pm	2:00 pm
2:15 pm	2:15 pm	2:15 pm
2:30 pm	2:30 pm	2:30 pm
2:45 pm	2:45 pm	2:45 pm
3:00 pm	3:00 pm	3:00 pm
3:15 pm	3:15 pm	3:15 pm
3:30 pm	3:30 pm	3:30 pm
3:45 pm	3:45 pm	3:45 pm
4:00 pm	4:00 pm	4:00 pm
4:15 pm	4:15 pm	4:15 pm
4:30 pm	4:30 pm	4:30 pm
4:45 pm	4:45 pm	4:45 pm
5:00 pm	5:00 pm	5:00 pm
5:15 pm	5:15 pm	5:15 pm
5:30 pm	5:30 pm	5:30 pm
5:45 pm	5:45 pm	5:45 pm
6:00 pm	6:00 pm	6:00 pm

TIME MANAGEMENT

PERSONAL DEVELOPMENT	INSPECT	JOB DESCRIPTION	CREATE MAGIC!

Date _____   Date _____   Date _____

THURSDAY		FRIDAY		SATURDAY	
8:00 am		8:00 am			
8:15 am		8:15 am			
8:30 am		8:30 am			
8:45 am		8:45 am			
9:00 am		9:00 am			
9:15 am		9:15 am			
9:30 am		9:30 am			
9:45 am		9:45 am			
10:00 am		10:00 am			
10:15 am		10:15 am			
10:30 am		10:30 am			
10:45 am		10:45 am			
11:00 am		11:00 am			
11:15 am		11:15 am			
11:30 am		11:30 am			
11:45 am		11:45 am			
12:00 pm		12:00 pm			
12:15 pm		12:15 pm			
12:30 pm		12:30 pm			
12:45 pm		12:45 pm			
1:00 pm		1:00 pm			

				SUNDAY	
1:15 pm		1:15 pm			
1:30 pm		1:30 pm			
1:45 pm		1:45 pm			
2:00 pm		2:00 pm			
2:15 pm		2:15 pm			
2:30 pm		2:30 pm			
2:45 pm		2:45 pm			
3:00 pm		3:00 pm			
3:15 pm		3:15 pm			
3:30 pm		3:30 pm			
3:45 pm		3:45 pm			
4:00 pm		4:00 pm			
4:15 pm		4:15 pm			
4:30 pm		4:30 pm			
4:45 pm		4:45 pm			
5:00 pm		5:00 pm			
5:15 pm		5:15 pm			
5:30 pm		5:30 pm			
5:45 pm		5:45 pm			
6:00 pm		6:00 pm			

TIME MANAGEMENT

PERSONAL DEVELOPMENT	INSPECT	JOB DESCRIPTION	CREATE MAGIC!

Date _____

MONDAY

8:00 am	
8:15 am	
8:30 am	
8:45 am	
9:00 am	
9:15 am	
9:30 am	
9:45 am	
10:00 am	
10:15 am	
10:30 am	
10:45 am	
11:00 am	
11:15 am	
11:30 am	
11:45 am	
12:00 pm	
12:15 pm	
12:30 pm	
12:45 pm	
1:00 pm	
1:15 pm	
1:30 pm	
1:45 pm	
2:00 pm	
2:15 pm	
2:30 pm	
2:45 pm	
3:00 pm	
3:15 pm	
3:30 pm	
3:45 pm	
4:00 pm	
4:15 pm	
4:30 pm	
4:45 pm	
5:00 pm	
5:15 pm	
5:30 pm	
5:45 pm	
6:00 pm	

Date _____

TUESDAY

8:00 am	
8:15 am	
8:30 am	
8:45 am	
9:00 am	
9:15 am	
9:30 am	
9:45 am	
10:00 am	
10:15 am	
10:30 am	
10:45 am	
11:00 am	
11:15 am	
11:30 am	
11:45 am	
12:00 pm	
12:15 pm	
12:30 pm	
12:45 pm	
1:00 pm	
1:15 pm	
1:30 pm	
1:45 pm	
2:00 pm	
2:15 pm	
2:30 pm	
2:45 pm	
3:00 pm	
3:15 pm	
3:30 pm	
3:45 pm	
4:00 pm	
4:15 pm	
4:30 pm	
4:45 pm	
5:00 pm	
5:15 pm	
5:30 pm	
5:45 pm	
6:00 pm	

Date _____

WEDNESDAY

8:00 am	
8:15 am	
8:30 am	
8:45 am	
9:00 am	
9:15 am	
9:30 am	
9:45 am	
10:00 am	
10:15 am	
10:30 am	
10:45 am	
11:00 am	
11:15 am	
11:30 am	
11:45 am	
12:00 pm	
12:15 pm	
12:30 pm	
12:45 pm	
1:00 pm	
1:15 pm	
1:30 pm	
1:45 pm	
2:00 pm	
2:15 pm	
2:30 pm	
2:45 pm	
3:00 pm	
3:15 pm	
3:30 pm	
3:45 pm	
4:00 pm	
4:15 pm	
4:30 pm	
4:45 pm	
5:00 pm	
5:15 pm	
5:30 pm	
5:45 pm	
6:00 pm	

TIME MANAGEMENT

PERSONAL DEVELOPMENT	INSPECT	JOB DESCRIPTION	CREATE MAGIC!

Date _____

Date _____

Date _____

THURSDAY

8:00 am	
8:15 am	
8:30 am	
8:45 am	
9:00 am	
9:15 am	
9:30 am	
9:45 am	
10:00 am	
10:15 am	
10:30 am	
10:45 am	
11:00 am	
11:15 am	
11:30 am	
11:45 am	
12:00 pm	
12:15 pm	
12:30 pm	
12:45 pm	
1:00 pm	
1:15 pm	
1:30 pm	
1:45 pm	
2:00 pm	
2:15 pm	
2:30 pm	
2:45 pm	
3:00 pm	
3:15 pm	
3:30 pm	
3:45 pm	
4:00 pm	
4:15 pm	
4:30 pm	
4:45 pm	
5:00 pm	
5:15 pm	
5:30 pm	
5:45 pm	
6:00 pm	

FRIDAY

8:00 am	
8:15 am	
8:30 am	
8:45 am	
9:00 am	
9:15 am	
9:30 am	
9:45 am	
10:00 am	
10:15 am	
10:30 am	
10:45 am	
11:00 am	
11:15 am	
11:30 am	
11:45 am	
12:00 pm	
12:15 pm	
12:30 pm	
12:45 pm	
1:00 pm	
1:15 pm	
1:30 pm	
1:45 pm	
2:00 pm	
2:15 pm	
2:30 pm	
2:45 pm	
3:00 pm	
3:15 pm	
3:30 pm	
3:45 pm	
4:00 pm	
4:15 pm	
4:30 pm	
4:45 pm	
5:00 pm	
5:15 pm	
5:30 pm	
5:45 pm	
6:00 pm	

SATURDAY

SUNDAY

TIME MANAGEMENT

PERSONAL DEVELOPMENT	INSPECT	JOB DESCRIPTION	CREATE MAGIC!

Date _____   Date _____   Date _____

MONDAY	TUESDAY	WEDNESDAY
8:00 am	8:00 am	8:00 am
8:15 am	8:15 am	8:15 am
8:30 am	8:30 am	8:30 am
8:45 am	8:45 am	8:45 am
9:00 am	9:00 am	9:00 am
9:15 am	9:15 am	9:15 am
9:30 am	9:30 am	9:30 am
9:45 am	9:45 am	9:45 am
10:00 am	10:00 am	10:00 am
10:15 am	10:15 am	10:15 am
10:30 am	10:30 am	10:30 am
10:45 am	10:45 am	10:45 am
11:00 am	11:00 am	11:00 am
11:15 am	11:15 am	11:15 am
11:30 am	11:30 am	11:30 am
11:45 am	11:45 am	11:45 am
12:00 pm	12:00 pm	12:00 pm
12:15 pm	12:15 pm	12:15 pm
12:30 pm	12:30 pm	12:30 pm
12:45 pm	12:45 pm	12:45 pm
1:00 pm	1:00 pm	1:00 pm
1:15 pm	1:15 pm	1:15 pm
1:30 pm	1:30 pm	1:30 pm
1:45 pm	1:45 pm	1:45 pm
2:00 pm	2:00 pm	2:00 pm
2:15 pm	2:15 pm	2:15 pm
2:30 pm	2:30 pm	2:30 pm
2:45 pm	2:45 pm	2:45 pm
3:00 pm	3:00 pm	3:00 pm
3:15 pm	3:15 pm	3:15 pm
3:30 pm	3:30 pm	3:30 pm
3:45 pm	3:45 pm	3:45 pm
4:00 pm	4:00 pm	4:00 pm
4:15 pm	4:15 pm	4:15 pm
4:30 pm	4:30 pm	4:30 pm
4:45 pm	4:45 pm	4:45 pm
5:00 pm	5:00 pm	5:00 pm
5:15 pm	5:15 pm	5:15 pm
5:30 pm	5:30 pm	5:30 pm
5:45 pm	5:45 pm	5:45 pm
6:00 pm	6:00 pm	6:00 pm

TIME MANAGEMENT

PERSONAL DEVELOPMENT	INSPECT	JOB DESCRIPTION	CREATE MAGIC!

Date _____   Date _____   Date _____

THURSDAY		FRIDAY		SATURDAY	
8:00 am		8:00 am			
8:15 am		8:15 am			
8:30 am		8:30 am			
8:45 am		8:45 am			
9:00 am		9:00 am			
9:15 am		9:15 am			
9:30 am		9:30 am			
9:45 am		9:45 am			
10:00 am		10:00 am			
10:15 am		10:15 am			
10:30 am		10:30 am			
10:45 am		10:45 am			
11:00 am		11:00 am			
11:15 am		11:15 am			
11:30 am		11:30 am			
11:45 am		11:45 am			
12:00 pm		12:00 pm			
12:15 pm		12:15 pm			
12:30 pm		12:30 pm			
12:45 pm		12:45 pm			
1:00 pm		1:00 pm			

SUNDAY	

THURSDAY (cont.)		FRIDAY (cont.)		SUNDAY	
1:15 pm		1:15 pm			
1:30 pm		1:30 pm			
1:45 pm		1:45 pm			
2:00 pm		2:00 pm			
2:15 pm		2:15 pm			
2:30 pm		2:30 pm			
2:45 pm		2:45 pm			
3:00 pm		3:00 pm			
3:15 pm		3:15 pm			
3:30 pm		3:30 pm			
3:45 pm		3:45 pm			
4:00 pm		4:00 pm			
4:15 pm		4:15 pm			
4:30 pm		4:30 pm			
4:45 pm		4:45 pm			
5:00 pm		5:00 pm			
5:15 pm		5:15 pm			
5:30 pm		5:30 pm			
5:45 pm		5:45 pm			
6:00 pm		6:00 pm			

TIME MANAGEMENT

PERSONAL DEVELOPMENT	INSPECT	JOB DESCRIPTION	CREATE MAGIC!

Date _____   Date _____   Date _____

MONDAY	TUESDAY	WEDNESDAY
8:00 am	8:00 am	8:00 am
8:15 am	8:15 am	8:15 am
8:30 am	8:30 am	8:30 am
8:45 am	8:45 am	8:45 am
9:00 am	9:00 am	9:00 am
9:15 am	9:15 am	9:15 am
9:30 am	9:30 am	9:30 am
9:45 am	9:45 am	9:45 am
10:00 am	10:00 am	10:00 am
10:15 am	10:15 am	10:15 am
10:30 am	10:30 am	10:30 am
10:45 am	10:45 am	10:45 am
11:00 am	11:00 am	11:00 am
11:15 am	11:15 am	11:15 am
11:30 am	11:30 am	11:30 am
11:45 am	11:45 am	11:45 am
12:00 pm	12:00 pm	12:00 pm
12:15 pm	12:15 pm	12:15 pm
12:30 pm	12:30 pm	12:30 pm
12:45 pm	12:45 pm	12:45 pm
1:00 pm	1:00 pm	1:00 pm
1:15 pm	1:15 pm	1:15 pm
1:30 pm	1:30 pm	1:30 pm
1:45 pm	1:45 pm	1:45 pm
2:00 pm	2:00 pm	2:00 pm
2:15 pm	2:15 pm	2:15 pm
2:30 pm	2:30 pm	2:30 pm
2:45 pm	2:45 pm	2:45 pm
3:00 pm	3:00 pm	3:00 pm
3:15 pm	3:15 pm	3:15 pm
3:30 pm	3:30 pm	3:30 pm
3:45 pm	3:45 pm	3:45 pm
4:00 pm	4:00 pm	4:00 pm
4:15 pm	4:15 pm	4:15 pm
4:30 pm	4:30 pm	4:30 pm
4:45 pm	4:45 pm	4:45 pm
5:00 pm	5:00 pm	5:00 pm
5:15 pm	5:15 pm	5:15 pm
5:30 pm	5:30 pm	5:30 pm
5:45 pm	5:45 pm	5:45 pm
6:00 pm	6:00 pm	6:00 pm

TIME MANAGEMENT

PERSONAL DEVELOPMENT	INSPECT	JOB DESCRIPTION	CREATE MAGIC!

Date _____

Date _____

Date _____

THURSDAY	FRIDAY	SATURDAY
8:00 am	8:00 am	
8:15 am	8:15 am	
8:30 am	8:30 am	
8:45 am	8:45 am	
9:00 am	9:00 am	
9:15 am	9:15 am	
9:30 am	9:30 am	
9:45 am	9:45 am	
10:00 am	10:00 am	
10:15 am	10:15 am	
10:30 am	10:30 am	
10:45 am	10:45 am	
11:00 am	11:00 am	
11:15 am	11:15 am	
11:30 am	11:30 am	
11:45 am	11:45 am	
12:00 pm	12:00 pm	
12:15 pm	12:15 pm	
12:30 pm	12:30 pm	
12:45 pm	12:45 pm	
1:00 pm	1:00 pm	SUNDAY
1:15 pm	1:15 pm	
1:30 pm	1:30 pm	
1:45 pm	1:45 pm	
2:00 pm	2:00 pm	
2:15 pm	2:15 pm	
2:30 pm	2:30 pm	
2:45 pm	2:45 pm	
3:00 pm	3:00 pm	
3:15 pm	3:15 pm	
3:30 pm	3:30 pm	
3:45 pm	3:45 pm	
4:00 pm	4:00 pm	
4:15 pm	4:15 pm	
4:30 pm	4:30 pm	
4:45 pm	4:45 pm	
5:00 pm	5:00 pm	
5:15 pm	5:15 pm	
5:30 pm	5:30 pm	
5:45 pm	5:45 pm	
6:00 pm	6:00 pm	

TIME MANAGEMENT

PERSONAL DEVELOPMENT	INSPECT	JOB DESCRIPTION	CREATE MAGIC!

111

Date _____

MONDAY

8:00 am	
8:15 am	
8:30 am	
8:45 am	
9:00 am	
9:15 am	
9:30 am	
9:45 am	
10:00 am	
10:15 am	
10:30 am	
10:45 am	
11:00 am	
11:15 am	
11:30 am	
11:45 am	
12:00 pm	
12:15 pm	
12:30 pm	
12:45 pm	
1:00 pm	
1:15 pm	
1:30 pm	
1:45 pm	
2:00 pm	
2:15 pm	
2:30 pm	
2:45 pm	
3:00 pm	
3:15 pm	
3:30 pm	
3:45 pm	
4:00 pm	
4:15 pm	
4:30 pm	
4:45 pm	
5:00 pm	
5:15 pm	
5:30 pm	
5:45 pm	
6:00 pm	

Date _____

TUESDAY

8:00 am	
8:15 am	
8:30 am	
8:45 am	
9:00 am	
9:15 am	
9:30 am	
9:45 am	
10:00 am	
10:15 am	
10:30 am	
10:45 am	
11:00 am	
11:15 am	
11:30 am	
11:45 am	
12:00 pm	
12:15 pm	
12:30 pm	
12:45 pm	
1:00 pm	
1:15 pm	
1:30 pm	
1:45 pm	
2:00 pm	
2:15 pm	
2:30 pm	
2:45 pm	
3:00 pm	
3:15 pm	
3:30 pm	
3:45 pm	
4:00 pm	
4:15 pm	
4:30 pm	
4:45 pm	
5:00 pm	
5:15 pm	
5:30 pm	
5:45 pm	
6:00 pm	

Date _____

WEDNESDAY

8:00 am	
8:15 am	
8:30 am	
8:45 am	
9:00 am	
9:15 am	
9:30 am	
9:45 am	
10:00 am	
10:15 am	
10:30 am	
10:45 am	
11:00 am	
11:15 am	
11:30 am	
11:45 am	
12:00 pm	
12:15 pm	
12:30 pm	
12:45 pm	
1:00 pm	
1:15 pm	
1:30 pm	
1:45 pm	
2:00 pm	
2:15 pm	
2:30 pm	
2:45 pm	
3:00 pm	
3:15 pm	
3:30 pm	
3:45 pm	
4:00 pm	
4:15 pm	
4:30 pm	
4:45 pm	
5:00 pm	
5:15 pm	
5:30 pm	
5:45 pm	
6:00 pm	

TIME MANAGEMENT

PERSONAL DEVELOPMENT	INSPECT	JOB DESCRIPTION	CREATE MAGIC!

Date _____   Date _____   Date _____

THURSDAY	FRIDAY	SATURDAY

Time	Thursday	Time	Friday
8:00 am		8:00 am	
8:15 am		8:15 am	
8:30 am		8:30 am	
8:45 am		8:45 am	
9:00 am		9:00 am	
9:15 am		9:15 am	
9:30 am		9:30 am	
9:45 am		9:45 am	
10:00 am		10:00 am	
10:15 am		10:15 am	
10:30 am		10:30 am	
10:45 am		10:45 am	
11:00 am		11:00 am	
11:15 am		11:15 am	
11:30 am		11:30 am	
11:45 am		11:45 am	
12:00 pm		12:00 pm	
12:15 pm		12:15 pm	
12:30 pm		12:30 pm	
12:45 pm		12:45 pm	
1:00 pm		1:00 pm	
1:15 pm		1:15 pm	
1:30 pm		1:30 pm	
1:45 pm		1:45 pm	
2:00 pm		2:00 pm	
2:15 pm		2:15 pm	
2:30 pm		2:30 pm	
2:45 pm		2:45 pm	
3:00 pm		3:00 pm	
3:15 pm		3:15 pm	
3:30 pm		3:30 pm	
3:45 pm		3:45 pm	
4:00 pm		4:00 pm	
4:15 pm		4:15 pm	
4:30 pm		4:30 pm	
4:45 pm		4:45 pm	
5:00 pm		5:00 pm	
5:15 pm		5:15 pm	
5:30 pm		5:30 pm	
5:45 pm		5:45 pm	
6:00 pm		6:00 pm	

SUNDAY

TIME MANAGEMENT

PERSONAL DEVELOPMENT	INSPECT	JOB DESCRIPTION	CREATE MAGIC!

113

Date _____

Date _____

Date _____

MONDAY		TUESDAY		WEDNESDAY
8:00 am		8:00 am		8:00 am
8:15 am		8:15 am		8:15 am
8:30 am		8:30 am		8:30 am
8:45 am		8:45 am		8:45 am
9:00 am		9:00 am		9:00 am
9:15 am		9:15 am		9:15 am
9:30 am		9:30 am		9:30 am
9:45 am		9:45 am		9:45 am
10:00 am		10:00 am		10:00 am
10:15 am		10:15 am		10:15 am
10:30 am		10:30 am		10:30 am
10:45 am		10:45 am		10:45 am
11:00 am		11:00 am		11:00 am
11:15 am		11:15 am		11:15 am
11:30 am		11:30 am		11:30 am
11:45 am		11:45 am		11:45 am
12:00 pm		12:00 pm		12:00 pm
12:15 pm		12:15 pm		12:15 pm
12:30 pm		12:30 pm		12:30 pm
12:45 pm		12:45 pm		12:45 pm
1:00 pm		1:00 pm		1:00 pm
1:15 pm		1:15 pm		1:15 pm
1:30 pm		1:30 pm		1:30 pm
1:45 pm		1:45 pm		1:45 pm
2:00 pm		2:00 pm		2:00 pm
2:15 pm		2:15 pm		2:15 pm
2:30 pm		2:30 pm		2:30 pm
2:45 pm		2:45 pm		2:45 pm
3:00 pm		3:00 pm		3:00 pm
3:15 pm		3:15 pm		3:15 pm
3:30 pm		3:30 pm		3:30 pm
3:45 pm		3:45 pm		3:45 pm
4:00 pm		4:00 pm		4:00 pm
4:15 pm		4:15 pm		4:15 pm
4:30 pm		4:30 pm		4:30 pm
4:45 pm		4:45 pm		4:45 pm
5:00 pm		5:00 pm		5:00 pm
5:15 pm		5:15 pm		5:15 pm
5:30 pm		5:30 pm		5:30 pm
5:45 pm		5:45 pm		5:45 pm
6:00 pm		6:00 pm		6:00 pm

TIME MANAGEMENT

PERSONAL DEVELOPMENT	INSPECT	JOB DESCRIPTION	CREATE MAGIC!

Date _____

THURSDAY

8:00 am	
8:15 am	
8:30 am	
8:45 am	
9:00 am	
9:15 am	
9:30 am	
9:45 am	
10:00 am	
10:15 am	
10:30 am	
10:45 am	
11:00 am	
11:15 am	
11:30 am	
11:45 am	
12:00 pm	
12:15 pm	
12:30 pm	
12:45 pm	
1:00 pm	
1:15 pm	
1:30 pm	
1:45 pm	
2:00 pm	
2:15 pm	
2:30 pm	
2:45 pm	
3:00 pm	
3:15 pm	
3:30 pm	
3:45 pm	
4:00 pm	
4:15 pm	
4:30 pm	
4:45 pm	
5:00 pm	
5:15 pm	
5:30 pm	
5:45 pm	
6:00 pm	

Date _____

FRIDAY

8:00 am	
8:15 am	
8:30 am	
8:45 am	
9:00 am	
9:15 am	
9:30 am	
9:45 am	
10:00 am	
10:15 am	
10:30 am	
10:45 am	
11:00 am	
11:15 am	
11:30 am	
11:45 am	
12:00 pm	
12:15 pm	
12:30 pm	
12:45 pm	
1:00 pm	
1:15 pm	
1:30 pm	
1:45 pm	
2:00 pm	
2:15 pm	
2:30 pm	
2:45 pm	
3:00 pm	
3:15 pm	
3:30 pm	
3:45 pm	
4:00 pm	
4:15 pm	
4:30 pm	
4:45 pm	
5:00 pm	
5:15 pm	
5:30 pm	
5:45 pm	
6:00 pm	

Date _____

SATURDAY

SUNDAY

TIME MANAGEMENT

PERSONAL DEVELOPMENT	INSPECT	JOB DESCRIPTION	CREATE MAGIC!

115

Date _____

MONDAY

8:00 am	
8:15 am	
8:30 am	
8:45 am	
9:00 am	
9:15 am	
9:30 am	
9:45 am	
10:00 am	
10:15 am	
10:30 am	
10:45 am	
11:00 am	
11:15 am	
11:30 am	
11:45 am	
12:00 pm	
12:15 pm	
12:30 pm	
12:45 pm	
1:00 pm	
1:15 pm	
1:30 pm	
1:45 pm	
2:00 pm	
2:15 pm	
2:30 pm	
2:45 pm	
3:00 pm	
3:15 pm	
3:30 pm	
3:45 pm	
4:00 pm	
4:15 pm	
4:30 pm	
4:45 pm	
5:00 pm	
5:15 pm	
5:30 pm	
5:45 pm	
6:00 pm	

Date _____

TUESDAY

8:00 am	
8:15 am	
8:30 am	
8:45 am	
9:00 am	
9:15 am	
9:30 am	
9:45 am	
10:00 am	
10:15 am	
10:30 am	
10:45 am	
11:00 am	
11:15 am	
11:30 am	
11:45 am	
12:00 pm	
12:15 pm	
12:30 pm	
12:45 pm	
1:00 pm	
1:15 pm	
1:30 pm	
1:45 pm	
2:00 pm	
2:15 pm	
2:30 pm	
2:45 pm	
3:00 pm	
3:15 pm	
3:30 pm	
3:45 pm	
4:00 pm	
4:15 pm	
4:30 pm	
4:45 pm	
5:00 pm	
5:15 pm	
5:30 pm	
5:45 pm	
6:00 pm	

Date _____

WEDNESDAY

8:00 am	
8:15 am	
8:30 am	
8:45 am	
9:00 am	
9:15 am	
9:30 am	
9:45 am	
10:00 am	
10:15 am	
10:30 am	
10:45 am	
11:00 am	
11:15 am	
11:30 am	
11:45 am	
12:00 pm	
12:15 pm	
12:30 pm	
12:45 pm	
1:00 pm	
1:15 pm	
1:30 pm	
1:45 pm	
2:00 pm	
2:15 pm	
2:30 pm	
2:45 pm	
3:00 pm	
3:15 pm	
3:30 pm	
3:45 pm	
4:00 pm	
4:15 pm	
4:30 pm	
4:45 pm	
5:00 pm	
5:15 pm	
5:30 pm	
5:45 pm	
6:00 pm	

TIME MANAGEMENT

PERSONAL DEVELOPMENT	INSPECT	JOB DESCRIPTION	CREATE MAGIC!

Date _____   Date _____   Date _____

THURSDAY		FRIDAY		SATURDAY

8:00 am	
8:15 am	
8:30 am	
8:45 am	
9:00 am	
9:15 am	
9:30 am	
9:45 am	
10:00 am	
10:15 am	
10:30 am	
10:45 am	
11:00 am	
11:15 am	
11:30 am	
11:45 am	
12:00 pm	
12:15 pm	
12:30 pm	
12:45 pm	
1:00 pm	
1:15 pm	
1:30 pm	
1:45 pm	
2:00 pm	
2:15 pm	
2:30 pm	
2:45 pm	
3:00 pm	
3:15 pm	
3:30 pm	
3:45 pm	
4:00 pm	
4:15 pm	
4:30 pm	
4:45 pm	
5:00 pm	
5:15 pm	
5:30 pm	
5:45 pm	
6:00 pm	

FRIDAY column times:
8:00 am, 8:15 am, 8:30 am, 8:45 am, 9:00 am, 9:15 am, 9:30 am, 9:45 am, 10:00 am, 10:15 am, 10:30 am, 10:45 am, 11:00 am, 11:15 am, 11:30 am, 11:45 am, 12:00 pm, 12:15 pm, 12:30 pm, 12:45 pm, 1:00 pm, 1:15 pm, 1:30 pm, 1:45 pm, 2:00 pm, 2:15 pm, 2:30 pm, 2:45 pm, 3:00 pm, 3:15 pm, 3:30 pm, 3:45 pm, 4:00 pm, 4:15 pm, 4:30 pm, 4:45 pm, 5:00 pm, 5:15 pm, 5:30 pm, 5:45 pm, 6:00 pm

SUNDAY

TIME MANAGEMENT			
PERSONAL DEVELOPMENT	INSPECT	JOB DESCRIPTION	CREATE MAGIC!

117

Date _____ Date _____ Date _____

MONDAY	TUESDAY	WEDNESDAY
8:00 am	8:00 am	8:00 am
8:15 am	8:15 am	8:15 am
8:30 am	8:30 am	8:30 am
8:45 am	8:45 am	8:45 am
9:00 am	9:00 am	9:00 am
9:15 am	9:15 am	9:15 am
9:30 am	9:30 am	9:30 am
9:45 am	9:45 am	9:45 am
10:00 am	10:00 am	10:00 am
10:15 am	10:15 am	10:15 am
10:30 am	10:30 am	10:30 am
10:45 am	10:45 am	10:45 am
11:00 am	11:00 am	11:00 am
11:15 am	11:15 am	11:15 am
11:30 am	11:30 am	11:30 am
11:45 am	11:45 am	11:45 am
12:00 pm	12:00 pm	12:00 pm
12:15 pm	12:15 pm	12:15 pm
12:30 pm	12:30 pm	12:30 pm
12:45 pm	12:45 pm	12:45 pm
1:00 pm	1:00 pm	1:00 pm
1:15 pm	1:15 pm	1:15 pm
1:30 pm	1:30 pm	1:30 pm
1:45 pm	1:45 pm	1:45 pm
2:00 pm	2:00 pm	2:00 pm
2:15 pm	2:15 pm	2:15 pm
2:30 pm	2:30 pm	2:30 pm
2:45 pm	2:45 pm	2:45 pm
3:00 pm	3:00 pm	3:00 pm
3:15 pm	3:15 pm	3:15 pm
3:30 pm	3:30 pm	3:30 pm
3:45 pm	3:45 pm	3:45 pm
4:00 pm	4:00 pm	4:00 pm
4:15 pm	4:15 pm	4:15 pm
4:30 pm	4:30 pm	4:30 pm
4:45 pm	4:45 pm	4:45 pm
5:00 pm	5:00 pm	5:00 pm
5:15 pm	5:15 pm	5:15 pm
5:30 pm	5:30 pm	5:30 pm
5:45 pm	5:45 pm	5:45 pm
6:00 pm	6:00 pm	6:00 pm

TIME MANAGEMENT

PERSONAL DEVELOPMENT	INSPECT	JOB DESCRIPTION	CREATE MAGIC!

Date _____   Date _____   Date _____

THURSDAY		FRIDAY		SATURDAY
8:00 am		8:00 am		
8:15 am		8:15 am		
8:30 am		8:30 am		
8:45 am		8:45 am		
9:00 am		9:00 am		
9:15 am		9:15 am		
9:30 am		9:30 am		
9:45 am		9:45 am		
10:00 am		10:00 am		
10:15 am		10:15 am		
10:30 am		10:30 am		
10:45 am		10:45 am		
11:00 am		11:00 am		
11:15 am		11:15 am		
11:30 am		11:30 am		
11:45 am		11:45 am		
12:00 pm		12:00 pm		
12:15 pm		12:15 pm		
12:30 pm		12:30 pm		
12:45 pm		12:45 pm		
1:00 pm		1:00 pm		SUNDAY
1:15 pm		1:15 pm		
1:30 pm		1:30 pm		
1:45 pm		1:45 pm		
2:00 pm		2:00 pm		
2:15 pm		2:15 pm		
2:30 pm		2:30 pm		
2:45 pm		2:45 pm		
3:00 pm		3:00 pm		
3:15 pm		3:15 pm		
3:30 pm		3:30 pm		
3:45 pm		3:45 pm		
4:00 pm		4:00 pm		
4:15 pm		4:15 pm		
4:30 pm		4:30 pm		
4:45 pm		4:45 pm		
5:00 pm		5:00 pm		
5:15 pm		5:15 pm		
5:30 pm		5:30 pm		
5:45 pm		5:45 pm		
6:00 pm		6:00 pm		

TIME MANAGEMENT

PERSONAL DEVELOPMENT	INSPECT	JOB DESCRIPTION	CREATE MAGIC!

119

Date _____

Date _____

Date _____

MONDAY	TUESDAY	WEDNESDAY
8:00 am	8:00 am	8:00 am
8:15 am	8:15 am	8:15 am
8:30 am	8:30 am	8:30 am
8:45 am	8:45 am	8:45 am
9:00 am	9:00 am	9:00 am
9:15 am	9:15 am	9:15 am
9:30 am	9:30 am	9:30 am
9:45 am	9:45 am	9:45 am
10:00 am	10:00 am	10:00 am
10:15 am	10:15 am	10:15 am
10:30 am	10:30 am	10:30 am
10:45 am	10:45 am	10:45 am
11:00 am	11:00 am	11:00 am
11:15 am	11:15 am	11:15 am
11:30 am	11:30 am	11:30 am
11:45 am	11:45 am	11:45 am
12:00 pm	12:00 pm	12:00 pm
12:15 pm	12:15 pm	12:15 pm
12:30 pm	12:30 pm	12:30 pm
12:45 pm	12:45 pm	12:45 pm
1:00 pm	1:00 pm	1:00 pm
1:15 pm	1:15 pm	1:15 pm
1:30 pm	1:30 pm	1:30 pm
1:45 pm	1:45 pm	1:45 pm
2:00 pm	2:00 pm	2:00 pm
2:15 pm	2:15 pm	2:15 pm
2:30 pm	2:30 pm	2:30 pm
2:45 pm	2:45 pm	2:45 pm
3:00 pm	3:00 pm	3:00 pm
3:15 pm	3:15 pm	3:15 pm
3:30 pm	3:30 pm	3:30 pm
3:45 pm	3:45 pm	3:45 pm
4:00 pm	4:00 pm	4:00 pm
4:15 pm	4:15 pm	4:15 pm
4:30 pm	4:30 pm	4:30 pm
4:45 pm	4:45 pm	4:45 pm
5:00 pm	5:00 pm	5:00 pm
5:15 pm	5:15 pm	5:15 pm
5:30 pm	5:30 pm	5:30 pm
5:45 pm	5:45 pm	5:45 pm
6:00 pm	6:00 pm	6:00 pm

TIME MANAGEMENT

PERSONAL DEVELOPMENT	INSPECT	JOB DESCRIPTION	CREATE MAGIC!

Date _____

THURSDAY

8:00 am	
8:15 am	
8:30 am	
8:45 am	
9:00 am	
9:15 am	
9:30 am	
9:45 am	
10:00 am	
10:15 am	
10:30 am	
10:45 am	
11:00 am	
11:15 am	
11:30 am	
11:45 am	
12:00 pm	
12:15 pm	
12:30 pm	
12:45 pm	
1:00 pm	
1:15 pm	
1:30 pm	
1:45 pm	
2:00 pm	
2:15 pm	
2:30 pm	
2:45 pm	
3:00 pm	
3:15 pm	
3:30 pm	
3:45 pm	
4:00 pm	
4:15 pm	
4:30 pm	
4:45 pm	
5:00 pm	
5:15 pm	
5:30 pm	
5:45 pm	
6:00 pm	

Date _____

FRIDAY

8:00 am	
8:15 am	
8:30 am	
8:45 am	
9:00 am	
9:15 am	
9:30 am	
9:45 am	
10:00 am	
10:15 am	
10:30 am	
10:45 am	
11:00 am	
11:15 am	
11:30 am	
11:45 am	
12:00 pm	
12:15 pm	
12:30 pm	
12:45 pm	
1:00 pm	
1:15 pm	
1:30 pm	
1:45 pm	
2:00 pm	
2:15 pm	
2:30 pm	
2:45 pm	
3:00 pm	
3:15 pm	
3:30 pm	
3:45 pm	
4:00 pm	
4:15 pm	
4:30 pm	
4:45 pm	
5:00 pm	
5:15 pm	
5:30 pm	
5:45 pm	
6:00 pm	

Date _____

SATURDAY

SUNDAY

TIME MANAGEMENT

PERSONAL DEVELOPMENT	INSPECT	JOB DESCRIPTION	CREATE MAGIC!

121

Date _____   Date _____   Date _____

MONDAY	TUESDAY	WEDNESDAY
8:00 am	8:00 am	8:00 am
8:15 am	8:15 am	8:15 am
8:30 am	8:30 am	8:30 am
8:45 am	8:45 am	8:45 am
9:00 am	9:00 am	9:00 am
9:15 am	9:15 am	9:15 am
9:30 am	9:30 am	9:30 am
9:45 am	9:45 am	9:45 am
10:00 am	10:00 am	10:00 am
10:15 am	10:15 am	10:15 am
10:30 am	10:30 am	10:30 am
10:45 am	10:45 am	10:45 am
11:00 am	11:00 am	11:00 am
11:15 am	11:15 am	11:15 am
11:30 am	11:30 am	11:30 am
11:45 am	11:45 am	11:45 am
12:00 pm	12:00 pm	12:00 pm
12:15 pm	12:15 pm	12:15 pm
12:30 pm	12:30 pm	12:30 pm
12:45 pm	12:45 pm	12:45 pm
1:00 pm	1:00 pm	1:00 pm
1:15 pm	1:15 pm	1:15 pm
1:30 pm	1:30 pm	1:30 pm
1:45 pm	1:45 pm	1:45 pm
2:00 pm	2:00 pm	2:00 pm
2:15 pm	2:15 pm	2:15 pm
2:30 pm	2:30 pm	2:30 pm
2:45 pm	2:45 pm	2:45 pm
3:00 pm	3:00 pm	3:00 pm
3:15 pm	3:15 pm	3:15 pm
3:30 pm	3:30 pm	3:30 pm
3:45 pm	3:45 pm	3:45 pm
4:00 pm	4:00 pm	4:00 pm
4:15 pm	4:15 pm	4:15 pm
4:30 pm	4:30 pm	4:30 pm
4:45 pm	4:45 pm	4:45 pm
5:00 pm	5:00 pm	5:00 pm
5:15 pm	5:15 pm	5:15 pm
5:30 pm	5:30 pm	5:30 pm
5:45 pm	5:45 pm	5:45 pm
6:00 pm	6:00 pm	6:00 pm

DAILY PLANNER

TIME MANAGEMENT

PERSONAL DEVELOPMENT	INSPECT	JOB DESCRIPTION	CREATE MAGIC!

122

Date _____

THURSDAY

8:00 am	
8:15 am	
8:30 am	
8:45 am	
9:00 am	
9:15 am	
9:30 am	
9:45 am	
10:00 am	
10:15 am	
10:30 am	
10:45 am	
11:00 am	
11:15 am	
11:30 am	
11:45 am	
12:00 pm	
12:15 pm	
12:30 pm	
12:45 pm	
1:00 pm	
1:15 pm	
1:30 pm	
1:45 pm	
2:00 pm	
2:15 pm	
2:30 pm	
2:45 pm	
3:00 pm	
3:15 pm	
3:30 pm	
3:45 pm	
4:00 pm	
4:15 pm	
4:30 pm	
4:45 pm	
5:00 pm	
5:15 pm	
5:30 pm	
5:45 pm	
6:00 pm	

Date _____

FRIDAY

8:00 am	
8:15 am	
8:30 am	
8:45 am	
9:00 am	
9:15 am	
9:30 am	
9:45 am	
10:00 am	
10:15 am	
10:30 am	
10:45 am	
11:00 am	
11:15 am	
11:30 am	
11:45 am	
12:00 pm	
12:15 pm	
12:30 pm	
12:45 pm	
1:00 pm	
1:15 pm	
1:30 pm	
1:45 pm	
2:00 pm	
2:15 pm	
2:30 pm	
2:45 pm	
3:00 pm	
3:15 pm	
3:30 pm	
3:45 pm	
4:00 pm	
4:15 pm	
4:30 pm	
4:45 pm	
5:00 pm	
5:15 pm	
5:30 pm	
5:45 pm	
6:00 pm	

Date _____

SATURDAY

SUNDAY

TIME MANAGEMENT

PERSONAL DEVELOPMENT	INSPECT	JOB DESCRIPTION	CREATE MAGIC!

Date _____   Date _____   Date _____

MONDAY	TUESDAY	WEDNESDAY
8:00 am	8:00 am	8:00 am
8:15 am	8:15 am	8:15 am
8:30 am	8:30 am	8:30 am
8:45 am	8:45 am	8:45 am
9:00 am	9:00 am	9:00 am
9:15 am	9:15 am	9:15 am
9:30 am	9:30 am	9:30 am
9:45 am	9:45 am	9:45 am
10:00 am	10:00 am	10:00 am
10:15 am	10:15 am	10:15 am
10:30 am	10:30 am	10:30 am
10:45 am	10:45 am	10:45 am
11:00 am	11:00 am	11:00 am
11:15 am	11:15 am	11:15 am
11:30 am	11:30 am	11:30 am
11:45 am	11:45 am	11:45 am
12:00 pm	12:00 pm	12:00 pm
12:15 pm	12:15 pm	12:15 pm
12:30 pm	12:30 pm	12:30 pm
12:45 pm	12:45 pm	12:45 pm
1:00 pm	1:00 pm	1:00 pm
1:15 pm	1:15 pm	1:15 pm
1:30 pm	1:30 pm	1:30 pm
1:45 pm	1:45 pm	1:45 pm
2:00 pm	2:00 pm	2:00 pm
2:15 pm	2:15 pm	2:15 pm
2:30 pm	2:30 pm	2:30 pm
2:45 pm	2:45 pm	2:45 pm
3:00 pm	3:00 pm	3:00 pm
3:15 pm	3:15 pm	3:15 pm
3:30 pm	3:30 pm	3:30 pm
3:45 pm	3:45 pm	3:45 pm
4:00 pm	4:00 pm	4:00 pm
4:15 pm	4:15 pm	4:15 pm
4:30 pm	4:30 pm	4:30 pm
4:45 pm	4:45 pm	4:45 pm
5:00 pm	5:00 pm	5:00 pm
5:15 pm	5:15 pm	5:15 pm
5:30 pm	5:30 pm	5:30 pm
5:45 pm	5:45 pm	5:45 pm
6:00 pm	6:00 pm	6:00 pm

TIME MANAGEMENT

PERSONAL DEVELOPMENT	INSPECT	JOB DESCRIPTION	CREATE MAGIC!

Date _____

Date _____

Date _____

THURSDAY		FRIDAY		SATURDAY	
8:00 am		8:00 am			
8:15 am		8:15 am			
8:30 am		8:30 am			
8:45 am		8:45 am			
9:00 am		9:00 am			
9:15 am		9:15 am			
9:30 am		9:30 am			
9:45 am		9:45 am			
10:00 am		10:00 am			
10:15 am		10:15 am			
10:30 am		10:30 am			
10:45 am		10:45 am			
11:00 am		11:00 am			
11:15 am		11:15 am			
11:30 am		11:30 am			
11:45 am		11:45 am			
12:00 pm		12:00 pm			
12:15 pm		12:15 pm			
12:30 pm		12:30 pm			
12:45 pm		12:45 pm			
1:00 pm		1:00 pm		SUNDAY	
1:15 pm		1:15 pm			
1:30 pm		1:30 pm			
1:45 pm		1:45 pm			
2:00 pm		2:00 pm			
2:15 pm		2:15 pm			
2:30 pm		2:30 pm			
2:45 pm		2:45 pm			
3:00 pm		3:00 pm			
3:15 pm		3:15 pm			
3:30 pm		3:30 pm			
3:45 pm		3:45 pm			
4:00 pm		4:00 pm			
4:15 pm		4:15 pm			
4:30 pm		4:30 pm			
4:45 pm		4:45 pm			
5:00 pm		5:00 pm			
5:15 pm		5:15 pm			
5:30 pm		5:30 pm			
5:45 pm		5:45 pm			
6:00 pm		6:00 pm			

TIME MANAGEMENT

PERSONAL DEVELOPMENT	INSPECT	JOB DESCRIPTION	CREATE MAGIC!

125

Date _____

MONDAY

8:00 am	
8:15 am	
8:30 am	
8:45 am	
9:00 am	
9:15 am	
9:30 am	
9:45 am	
10:00 am	
10:15 am	
10:30 am	
10:45 am	
11:00 am	
11:15 am	
11:30 am	
11:45 am	
12:00 pm	
12:15 pm	
12:30 pm	
12:45 pm	
1:00 pm	
1:15 pm	
1:30 pm	
1:45 pm	
2:00 pm	
2:15 pm	
2:30 pm	
2:45 pm	
3:00 pm	
3:15 pm	
3:30 pm	
3:45 pm	
4:00 pm	
4:15 pm	
4:30 pm	
4:45 pm	
5:00 pm	
5:15 pm	
5:30 pm	
5:45 pm	
6:00 pm	

Date _____

TUESDAY

8:00 am	
8:15 am	
8:30 am	
8:45 am	
9:00 am	
9:15 am	
9:30 am	
9:45 am	
10:00 am	
10:15 am	
10:30 am	
10:45 am	
11:00 am	
11:15 am	
11:30 am	
11:45 am	
12:00 pm	
12:15 pm	
12:30 pm	
12:45 pm	
1:00 pm	
1:15 pm	
1:30 pm	
1:45 pm	
2:00 pm	
2:15 pm	
2:30 pm	
2:45 pm	
3:00 pm	
3:15 pm	
3:30 pm	
3:45 pm	
4:00 pm	
4:15 pm	
4:30 pm	
4:45 pm	
5:00 pm	
5:15 pm	
5:30 pm	
5:45 pm	
6:00 pm	

Date _____

WEDNESDAY

8:00 am	
8:15 am	
8:30 am	
8:45 am	
9:00 am	
9:15 am	
9:30 am	
9:45 am	
10:00 am	
10:15 am	
10:30 am	
10:45 am	
11:00 am	
11:15 am	
11:30 am	
11:45 am	
12:00 pm	
12:15 pm	
12:30 pm	
12:45 pm	
1:00 pm	
1:15 pm	
1:30 pm	
1:45 pm	
2:00 pm	
2:15 pm	
2:30 pm	
2:45 pm	
3:00 pm	
3:15 pm	
3:30 pm	
3:45 pm	
4:00 pm	
4:15 pm	
4:30 pm	
4:45 pm	
5:00 pm	
5:15 pm	
5:30 pm	
5:45 pm	
6:00 pm	

TIME MANAGEMENT

PERSONAL DEVELOPMENT	INSPECT	JOB DESCRIPTION	CREATE MAGIC!

Date _____

THURSDAY

8:00 am	
8:15 am	
8:30 am	
8:45 am	
9:00 am	
9:15 am	
9:30 am	
9:45 am	
10:00 am	
10:15 am	
10:30 am	
10:45 am	
11:00 am	
11:15 am	
11:30 am	
11:45 am	
12:00 pm	
12:15 pm	
12:30 pm	
12:45 pm	
1:00 pm	
1:15 pm	
1:30 pm	
1:45 pm	
2:00 pm	
2:15 pm	
2:30 pm	
2:45 pm	
3:00 pm	
3:15 pm	
3:30 pm	
3:45 pm	
4:00 pm	
4:15 pm	
4:30 pm	
4:45 pm	
5:00 pm	
5:15 pm	
5:30 pm	
5:45 pm	
6:00 pm	

Date _____

FRIDAY

8:00 am	
8:15 am	
8:30 am	
8:45 am	
9:00 am	
9:15 am	
9:30 am	
9:45 am	
10:00 am	
10:15 am	
10:30 am	
10:45 am	
11:00 am	
11:15 am	
11:30 am	
11:45 am	
12:00 pm	
12:15 pm	
12:30 pm	
12:45 pm	
1:00 pm	
1:15 pm	
1:30 pm	
1:45 pm	
2:00 pm	
2:15 pm	
2:30 pm	
2:45 pm	
3:00 pm	
3:15 pm	
3:30 pm	
3:45 pm	
4:00 pm	
4:15 pm	
4:30 pm	
4:45 pm	
5:00 pm	
5:15 pm	
5:30 pm	
5:45 pm	
6:00 pm	

Date _____

SATURDAY

SUNDAY

TIME MANAGEMENT

PERSONAL DEVELOPMENT	INSPECT	JOB DESCRIPTION	CREATE MAGIC!

Date _____   Date _____   Date _____

MONDAY	TUESDAY	WEDNESDAY
8:00 am	8:00 am	8:00 am
8:15 am	8:15 am	8:15 am
8:30 am	8:30 am	8:30 am
8:45 am	8:45 am	8:45 am
9:00 am	9:00 am	9:00 am
9:15 am	9:15 am	9:15 am
9:30 am	9:30 am	9:30 am
9:45 am	9:45 am	9:45 am
10:00 am	10:00 am	10:00 am
10:15 am	10:15 am	10:15 am
10:30 am	10:30 am	10:30 am
10:45 am	10:45 am	10:45 am
11:00 am	11:00 am	11:00 am
11:15 am	11:15 am	11:15 am
11:30 am	11:30 am	11:30 am
11:45 am	11:45 am	11:45 am
12:00 pm	12:00 pm	12:00 pm
12:15 pm	12:15 pm	12:15 pm
12:30 pm	12:30 pm	12:30 pm
12:45 pm	12:45 pm	12:45 pm
1:00 pm	1:00 pm	1:00 pm
1:15 pm	1:15 pm	1:15 pm
1:30 pm	1:30 pm	1:30 pm
1:45 pm	1:45 pm	1:45 pm
2:00 pm	2:00 pm	2:00 pm
2:15 pm	2:15 pm	2:15 pm
2:30 pm	2:30 pm	2:30 pm
2:45 pm	2:45 pm	2:45 pm
3:00 pm	3:00 pm	3:00 pm
3:15 pm	3:15 pm	3:15 pm
3:30 pm	3:30 pm	3:30 pm
3:45 pm	3:45 pm	3:45 pm
4:00 pm	4:00 pm	4:00 pm
4:15 pm	4:15 pm	4:15 pm
4:30 pm	4:30 pm	4:30 pm
4:45 pm	4:45 pm	4:45 pm
5:00 pm	5:00 pm	5:00 pm
5:15 pm	5:15 pm	5:15 pm
5:30 pm	5:30 pm	5:30 pm
5:45 pm	5:45 pm	5:45 pm
6:00 pm	6:00 pm	6:00 pm

TIME MANAGEMENT

PERSONAL DEVELOPMENT	INSPECT	JOB DESCRIPTION	CREATE MAGIC!

Date _____ Date _____ Date _____

THURSDAY	FRIDAY	SATURDAY
8:00 am	8:00 am	
8:15 am	8:15 am	
8:30 am	8:30 am	
8:45 am	8:45 am	
9:00 am	9:00 am	
9:15 am	9:15 am	
9:30 am	9:30 am	
9:45 am	9:45 am	
10:00 am	10:00 am	
10:15 am	10:15 am	
10:30 am	10:30 am	
10:45 am	10:45 am	
11:00 am	11:00 am	
11:15 am	11:15 am	
11:30 am	11:30 am	
11:45 am	11:45 am	
12:00 pm	12:00 pm	
12:15 pm	12:15 pm	
12:30 pm	12:30 pm	
12:45 pm	12:45 pm	
1:00 pm	1:00 pm	

SUNDAY

THURSDAY	FRIDAY	SUNDAY
1:15 pm	1:15 pm	
1:30 pm	1:30 pm	
1:45 pm	1:45 pm	
2:00 pm	2:00 pm	
2:15 pm	2:15 pm	
2:30 pm	2:30 pm	
2:45 pm	2:45 pm	
3:00 pm	3:00 pm	
3:15 pm	3:15 pm	
3:30 pm	3:30 pm	
3:45 pm	3:45 pm	
4:00 pm	4:00 pm	
4:15 pm	4:15 pm	
4:30 pm	4:30 pm	
4:45 pm	4:45 pm	
5:00 pm	5:00 pm	
5:15 pm	5:15 pm	
5:30 pm	5:30 pm	
5:45 pm	5:45 pm	
6:00 pm	6:00 pm	

TIME MANAGEMENT

PERSONAL DEVELOPMENT	INSPECT	JOB DESCRIPTION	CREATE MAGIC!

BE A PLANNER

WORKSHEETS

WORKSHEET:
POWER HOUR

Do this worksheet daily

How do you eat an elephant? One bite at a time! The power hour will help you reach your goals this year. It's one hour set aside each day to manage your FOCUS.

This book includes 80 Power Hour Worksheets; you can download extras at *www.tinablack.net* (use the access code **BE**).

How it works: Set aside 30 minutes in the morning and 30 minutes before you go to bed.

Here's my routine:

MORNING:

- Wake up
- Make coffee
- Light my candle
- Play soft music
- Fill in my journal and the Power Hour Worksheet
- Bible study
- Plan my day

EVENING:

- Go through my schedule. Highlight what I completed and reschedule what I did not complete to another day
- Fill out the rest of my Power Hour Worksheet

P.S. I mentioned my journal in this routine. I hope you'll join me for my Authentic Journaling class, which I periodically offer in my online masterminds and workshops (available at *www.tinablack.net*).

POWER UP! (POWER HOUR)

TASK LIST

☐

☐

☐

☐

NOTES AND IDEAS
Fill Out In the Morning

PRAYERS

TODAY'S PRIORITIES
What will make today a win for you?

1)

2)

3)

DAILY REFLECTIONS

THIS MORNING I AM THANKFUL FOR...

1.

2.

3.

10 MINUTES TO
REFLECT ON YOUR DAY

Date:

Three moments you'd like to remember:

One idea from today that you'd like to explore further:

Your initial thoughts:

One of the day's challenges, big or small:

_____

_____

_____

Things you are grateful for today:

_____

_____

_____

_____

_____

Two events or news stories out in the world that caught your attention:

_____

_____

135

POWER HOUR WORKSHEET

POWER UP! (POWER HOUR)

TASK LIST

☐

☐

☐

☐

NOTES AND IDEAS
Fill Out In the Morning

PRAYERS

TODAY'S PRIORITIES
What will make today a win for you?

1)

2)

3)

DAILY REFLECTIONS

THIS MORNING I AM THANKFUL FOR...

1.

2.

3.

10 MINUTES TO
REFLECT ON YOUR DAY

Date:

Three moments you'd like to remember:

One idea from today that you'd like to explore further:

One of the day's challenges, big or small:

Your initial thoughts:

Things you are grateful for today:

Two events or news stories out in the world that caught your attention:

POWER UP! (POWER HOUR)

TASK LIST

☐

☐

☐

☐

NOTES AND IDEAS
Fill Out In the Morning

PRAYERS

TODAY'S PRIORITIES
What will make today a win for you?

1)

2)

3)

DAILY REFLECTIONS

THIS MORNING I AM THANKFUL FOR...

1.

2.

3.

10 MINUTES TO
REFLECT ON YOUR DAY

Date:

Three moments you'd like to remember:

One idea from today that you'd like to explore further:

One of the day's challenges, big or small:

Your initial thoughts:

Things you are grateful for today:

Two events or news stories out in the world that caught your attention:

POWER UP! (POWER HOUR)

TASK LIST

☐

☐

☐

☐

NOTES AND IDEAS
Fill Out In the Morning

PRAYERS

TODAY'S PRIORITIES
What will make today a win for you?

1)

2)

3)

DAILY REFLECTIONS

THIS MORNING I AM THANKFUL FOR...

1.

2.

3.

10 MINUTES TO
REFLECT ON YOUR DAY

Date:

Three moments you'd like to remember:

One idea from today that you'd like to explore further:

Your initial thoughts:

One of the day's challenges, big or small:

Things you are grateful for today:

Two events or news stories out in the world that caught your attention:

141

POWER UP! (POWER HOUR)

TASK LIST

☐

☐

☐

☐

NOTES AND IDEAS
Fill Out In the Morning

PRAYERS

TODAY'S PRIORITIES
What will make today a win for you?

1)

2)

3)

DAILY REFLECTIONS

THIS MORNING I AM THANKFUL FOR...

1.

2.

3.

10 MINUTES TO
REFLECT ON YOUR DAY

Date:

Three moments you'd like to remember:

One idea from today that you'd like to explore further:

Your initial thoughts:

One of the day's challenges, big or small:

_____

_____

_____

Things you are grateful for today:

_____

_____

_____

Two events or news stories out in the world that caught your attention:

_____

_____

_____

_____

_____

143

POWER UP! (POWER HOUR)

TASK LIST

☐

☐

☐

☐

NOTES AND IDEAS
Fill Out In the Morning

PRAYERS

TODAY'S PRIORITIES
What will make today a win for you?

1)

2)

3)

DAILY REFLECTIONS

THIS MORNING I AM THANKFUL FOR...

1.

2.

3.

10 MINUTES TO
REFLECT ON YOUR DAY

Date:

Three moments you'd like to remember:

One idea from today that you'd like to explore further:

Your initial thoughts:

One of the day's challenges, big or small:

_____
_____
_____

Things you are grateful for today:

_____
_____
_____
_____
_____

Two events or news stories out in the world that caught your attention:

_____
_____

145

POWER UP! (POWER HOUR)

TASK LIST

☐

☐

☐

☐

NOTES AND IDEAS
Fill Out In the Morning

PRAYERS

TODAY'S PRIORITIES
What will make today a win for you?

1)

2)

3)

DAILY REFLECTIONS

THIS MORNING I AM THANKFUL FOR...

1.

2.

3.

10 MINUTES TO
REFLECT ON YOUR DAY

Date:

Three moments you'd like to remember:

One idea from today that you'd like to explore further:

Your initial thoughts:

One of the day's challenges, big or small:

Things you are grateful for today:

Two events or news stories out in the world that caught your attention:

POWER HOUR WORKSHEET

POWER UP! (POWER HOUR)

TASK LIST

☐

☐

☐

☐

NOTES AND IDEAS
Fill Out In the Morning

PRAYERS

TODAY'S PRIORITIES
What will make today a win for you?

1)

2)

3)

DAILY REFLECTIONS

THIS MORNING I AM THANKFUL FOR...

1.

2.

3.

10 MINUTES TO
REFLECT ON YOUR DAY

Date:

Three moments you'd like to remember:

One idea from today that you'd like to explore further:

Your initial thoughts:

One of the day's challenges, big or small:

_____
_____
_____

Things you are grateful for today:

_____
_____
_____
_____
_____

Two events or news stories out in the world that caught your attention:

_____
_____

DAILY

POWER UP! (POWER HOUR)

TASK LIST

☐

☐

☐

☐

NOTES AND IDEAS
Fill Out In the Morning

PRAYERS

TODAY'S PRIORITIES
What will make today a win for you?

1)

2)

3)

DAILY REFLECTIONS

THIS MORNING I AM THANKFUL FOR...

1.

2.

3.

10 MINUTES TO
REFLECT ON YOUR DAY

Date:

Three moments you'd like to remember:

One idea from today that you'd like to explore further:

One of the day's challenges, big or small:

Your initial thoughts:

Things you are grateful for today:

Two events or news stories out in the world that caught your attention:

DAILY

POWER UP! (POWER HOUR)

TASK LIST

☐

☐

☐

☐

NOTES AND IDEAS
Fill Out In the Morning

PRAYERS

TODAY'S PRIORITIES
What will make today a win for you?

1)

2)

3)

DAILY REFLECTIONS

THIS MORNING I AM THANKFUL FOR...

1.

2.

3.

10 MINUTES TO
REFLECT ON YOUR DAY

Date:

Three moments you'd like to remember:

One idea from today that you'd like to explore further:

Your initial thoughts:

One of the day's challenges, big or small:

Things you are grateful for today:

Two events or news stories out in the world that caught your attention:

POWER UP! (POWER HOUR)

TASK LIST

- [ ]
- [ ]
- [ ]
- [ ]

NOTES AND IDEAS
Fill Out In the Morning

PRAYERS

TODAY'S PRIORITIES
What will make today a win for you?

1)

2)

3)

DAILY REFLECTIONS

THIS MORNING I AM THANKFUL FOR...

1.

2.

3.

DAILY

10 MINUTES TO
REFLECT ON YOUR DAY

Date:

Three moments you'd like to remember:

One idea from today that you'd like to explore further:

Your initial thoughts:

One of the day's challenges, big or small:

Things you are grateful for today:

Two events or news stories out in the world that caught your attention:

POWER UP! (POWER HOUR)

TASK LIST

☐

☐

☐

☐

NOTES AND IDEAS
Fill Out In the Morning

PRAYERS

TODAY'S PRIORITIES
What will make today a win for you?

1)

2)

3)

DAILY REFLECTIONS

THIS MORNING I AM THANKFUL FOR...
1.
2.
3.

10 MINUTES TO
REFLECT ON YOUR DAY

Date:

Three moments you'd like to remember:

One idea from today that you'd like to explore further:

Your initial thoughts:

Two events or news stories out in the world that caught your attention:

One of the day's challenges, big or small:

Things you are grateful for today:

157

DAILY

POWER UP! (POWER HOUR)

TASK LIST

☐

☐

☐

☐

NOTES AND IDEAS
Fill Out In the Morning

PRAYERS

TODAY'S PRIORITIES
What will make today a win for you?

1)

2)

3)

DAILY REFLECTIONS

THIS MORNING I AM THANKFUL FOR...

1.

2.

3.

10 MINUTES TO
REFLECT ON YOUR DAY

Date:

Three moments you'd like to remember:

One idea from today that you'd like to explore further:

Your initial thoughts:

One of the day's challenges, big or small:

Things you are grateful for today:

Two events or news stories out in the world that caught your attention:

159

POWER UP! (POWER HOUR)

TASK LIST

- [ ]
- [ ]
- [ ]
- [ ]

NOTES AND IDEAS
Fill Out In the Morning

PRAYERS

TODAY'S PRIORITIES
What will make today a win for you?

1)

2)

3)

DAILY REFLECTIONS

THIS MORNING I AM THANKFUL FOR...

1.

2.

3.

160

10 MINUTES TO
REFLECT ON YOUR DAY

Date:

Three moments you'd like to remember:

One idea from today that you'd like to explore further:

Your initial thoughts:

One of the day's challenges, big or small:

_____
_____
_____

Things you are grateful for today:

_____
_____
_____
_____

Two events or news stories out in the world that caught your attention:

_____
_____

161

DAILY

POWER UP! (POWER HOUR)

TASK LIST

- [ ]
- [ ]
- [ ]
- [ ]

NOTES AND IDEAS
Fill Out In the Morning

PRAYERS

TODAY'S PRIORITIES
What will make today a win for you?

1)

2)

3)

DAILY REFLECTIONS

THIS MORNING I AM THANKFUL FOR...

1.

2.

3.

10 MINUTES TO
REFLECT ON YOUR DAY

Date:

Three moments you'd like to remember:

One idea from today that you'd like to explore further:

One of the day's challenges, big or small:

Your initial thoughts:

Things you are grateful for today:

Two events or news stories out in the world that caught your attention:

163

DAILY

POWER UP! (POWER HOUR)

TASK LIST

☐

☐

☐

☐

NOTES AND IDEAS
Fill Out In the Morning

PRAYERS

TODAY'S PRIORITIES
What will make today a win for you?

1)

2)

3)

DAILY REFLECTIONS

THIS MORNING I AM THANKFUL FOR...

1.

2.

3.

10 MINUTES TO
REFLECT ON YOUR DAY

Date:

Three moments you'd like to remember:

One idea from today that you'd like to explore further:

Your initial thoughts:

One of the day's challenges, big or small:

Things you are grateful for today:

Two events or news stories out in the world that caught your attention:

DAILY

POWER UP! (POWER HOUR)

TASK LIST

- [ ]
- [ ]
- [ ]
- [ ]

NOTES AND IDEAS
Fill Out In the Morning

PRAYERS

TODAY'S PRIORITIES
What will make today a win for you?

1)

2)

3)

DAILY REFLECTIONS

THIS MORNING I AM THANKFUL FOR...

1.

2.

3.

10 MINUTES TO
REFLECT ON YOUR DAY

Date:

Three moments you'd like to remember:

One idea from today that you'd like to explore further:

Your initial thoughts:

Two events or news stories out in the world that caught your attention:

_____

_____

One of the day's challenges, big or small:

_____
_____
_____

Things you are grateful for today:

_____
_____
_____
_____
_____
_____

POWER UP! (POWER HOUR)

TASK LIST

- [ ]
- [ ]
- [ ]
- [ ]

NOTES AND IDEAS
Fill Out In the Morning

PRAYERS

TODAY'S PRIORITIES
What will make today a win for you?

1)

2)

3)

DAILY REFLECTIONS

THIS MORNING I AM THANKFUL FOR...

1.

2.

3.

168

10 MINUTES TO
REFLECT ON YOUR DAY

Date:

Three moments you'd like to remember:

One idea from today that you'd like to explore further:

One of the day's challenges, big or small:

Your initial thoughts:

Things you are grateful for today:

Two events or news stories out in the world that caught your attention:

POWER UP! (POWER HOUR)

TASK LIST

☐

☐

☐

☐

NOTES AND IDEAS
Fill Out In the Morning

PRAYERS

TODAY'S PRIORITIES
What will make today a win for you?

1)

2)

3)

DAILY REFLECTIONS

THIS MORNING I AM THANKFUL FOR...

1.

2.

3.

10 MINUTES TO
REFLECT ON YOUR DAY

Date:

Three moments you'd like to remember:

One idea from today that you'd like to explore further:

Your initial thoughts:

One of the day's challenges, big or small:

_____
_____
_____

Things you are grateful for today:

_____
_____
_____
_____

Two events or news stories out in the world that caught your attention:

_____
_____

POWER UP! (POWER HOUR)

TASK LIST

☐

☐

☐

☐

NOTES AND IDEAS
Fill Out In the Morning

PRAYERS

TODAY'S PRIORITIES
What will make today a win for you?

1)

2)

3)

DAILY REFLECTIONS

THIS MORNING I AM THANKFUL FOR...

1.

2.

3.

10 MINUTES TO
REFLECT ON YOUR DAY

Date:

Three moments you'd like to remember:

One idea from today that you'd like to explore further:

Your initial thoughts:

One of the day's challenges, big or small:

Things you are grateful for today:

Two events or news stories out in the world that caught your attention:

POWER UP! (POWER HOUR)

TASK LIST

☐

☐

☐

☐

NOTES AND IDEAS
Fill Out In the Morning

PRAYERS

TODAY'S PRIORITIES
What will make today a win for you?

1)

2)

3)

DAILY REFLECTIONS

THIS MORNING I AM THANKFUL FOR...

1.

2.

3.

10 MINUTES TO
REFLECT ON YOUR DAY

Date:

Three moments you'd like to remember:

One idea from today that you'd like to explore further:

Your initial thoughts:

One of the day's challenges, big or small:

_____

_____

_____

Things you are grateful for today:

_____

_____

_____

Two events or news stories out in the world that caught your attention:

_____

_____

_____

_____

POWER UP! (POWER HOUR)

TASK LIST

☐

☐

☐

☐

NOTES AND IDEAS
Fill Out In the Morning

PRAYERS

TODAY'S PRIORITIES
What will make today a win for you?

1)

2)

3)

DAILY REFLECTIONS

THIS MORNING I AM THANKFUL FOR...

1.

2.

3.

10 MINUTES TO
REFLECT ON YOUR DAY

Date:

Three moments you'd like to remember:

One of the day's challenges, big or small:

_____

_____

_____

One idea from today that you'd like to explore further:

Your initial thoughts:

Things you are grateful for today:

_____

_____

_____

Two events or news stories out in the world that caught your attention:

_____

_____

_____

POWER UP! (POWER HOUR)

TASK LIST

☐

☐

☐

☐

NOTES AND IDEAS
Fill Out In the Morning

PRAYERS

TODAY'S PRIORITIES
What will make today a win for you?

1)

2)

3)

DAILY REFLECTIONS

THIS MORNING I AM THANKFUL FOR...

1.

2.

3.

10 MINUTES TO
REFLECT ON YOUR DAY

Date:

Three moments you'd like to remember:

One idea from today that you'd like to explore further:

One of the day's challenges, big or small:

Your initial thoughts:

Things you are grateful for today:

Two events or news stories out in the world that caught your attention:

DAILY

POWER UP! (POWER HOUR)

TASK LIST

☐

☐

☐

☐

NOTES AND IDEAS
Fill Out In the Morning

PRAYERS

TODAY'S PRIORITIES
What will make today a win for you?

1)

2)

3)

DAILY REFLECTIONS

THIS MORNING I AM THANKFUL FOR...
1.
2.
3.

10 MINUTES TO
REFLECT ON YOUR DAY

Date:

Three moments you'd like to remember:

One idea from today that you'd like to explore further:

One of the day's challenges, big or small:

Your initial thoughts:

Things you are grateful for today:

Two events or news stories out in the world that caught your attention:

DAILY

POWER UP! (POWER HOUR)

TASK LIST

☐

☐

☐

☐

NOTES AND IDEAS
Fill Out In the Morning

PRAYERS

TODAY'S PRIORITIES
What will make today a win for you?

1)

2)

3)

DAILY REFLECTIONS

THIS MORNING I AM THANKFUL FOR...

1.

2.

3.

10 MINUTES TO
REFLECT ON YOUR DAY

Date:

Three moments you'd like to remember:

One idea from today that you'd like to explore further:

One of the day's challenges, big or small:

Your initial thoughts:

Things you are grateful for today:

Two events or news stories out in the world that caught your attention:

183

POWER UP! (POWER HOUR)

TASK LIST

- [ ]
- [ ]
- [ ]
- [ ]

NOTES AND IDEAS
Fill Out In the Morning

PRAYERS

TODAY'S PRIORITIES
What will make today a win for you?

1)

2)

3)

DAILY REFLECTIONS

THIS MORNING I AM THANKFUL FOR...

1.

2.

3.

10 MINUTES TO
REFLECT ON YOUR DAY

Date:

Three moments you'd like to remember:

One idea from today that you'd like to explore further:

Your initial thoughts:

One of the day's challenges, big or small:

Things you are grateful for today:

Two events or news stories out in the world that caught your attention:

POWER UP! (POWER HOUR)

TASK LIST

☐

☐

☐

☐

NOTES AND IDEAS
Fill Out In the Morning

PRAYERS

TODAY'S PRIORITIES
What will make today a win for you?

1)

2)

3)

DAILY REFLECTIONS

THIS MORNING I AM THANKFUL FOR...

1.

2.

3.

10 MINUTES TO
REFLECT ON YOUR DAY

Date:

Three moments you'd like to remember:

One idea from today that you'd like to explore further:

One of the day's challenges, big or small:

Your initial thoughts:

Things you are grateful for today:

Two events or news stories out in the world that caught your attention:

187

DAILY

POWER UP! (POWER HOUR)

TASK LIST

- [ ]
- [ ]
- [ ]
- [ ]

NOTES AND IDEAS
Fill Out In the Morning

PRAYERS

TODAY'S PRIORITIES
What will make today a win for you?

1)

2)

3)

DAILY REFLECTIONS

THIS MORNING I AM THANKFUL FOR...

1.
2.
3.

10 MINUTES TO
REFLECT ON YOUR DAY

Date:

Three moments you'd like to remember:

One idea from today that you'd like to explore further:

Your initial thoughts:

One of the day's challenges, big or small:

_____

_____

_____

Things you are grateful for today:

_____

_____

_____

_____

_____

Two events or news stories out in the world that caught your attention:

_____

_____

189

POWER UP! (POWER HOUR)

TASK LIST

☐

☐

☐

☐

NOTES AND IDEAS
Fill Out In the Morning

PRAYERS

TODAY'S PRIORITIES
What will make today a win for you?

1)

2)

3)

DAILY REFLECTIONS

THIS MORNING I AM THANKFUL FOR...

1.

2.

3.

10 MINUTES TO
REFLECT ON YOUR DAY

Date:

Three moments you'd like to remember:

One idea from today that you'd like to explore further:

One of the day's challenges, big or small:

Your initial thoughts:

Things you are grateful for today:

Two events or news stories out in the world that caught your attention:

DAILY

POWER UP! (POWER HOUR)

TASK LIST

☐

☐

☐

☐

NOTES AND IDEAS
Fill Out In the Morning

PRAYERS

TODAY'S PRIORITIES
What will make today a win for you?

1)

2)

3)

DAILY REFLECTIONS

THIS MORNING I AM THANKFUL FOR...

1.

2.

3.

10 MINUTES TO
REFLECT ON YOUR DAY

Date:

Three moments you'd like to remember:

One idea from today that you'd like to explore further:

One of the day's challenges, big or small:

Your initial thoughts:

Things you are grateful for today:

Two events or news stories out in the world that caught your attention:

POWER UP! (POWER HOUR)

TASK LIST

☐

☐

☐

☐

NOTES AND IDEAS
Fill Out In the Morning

PRAYERS

TODAY'S PRIORITIES
What will make today a win for you?

1)

2)

3)

DAILY REFLECTIONS

THIS MORNING I AM THANKFUL FOR...

1.

2.

3.

10 MINUTES TO
REFLECT ON YOUR DAY

Date:

Three moments you'd like to remember:

One idea from today that you'd like to explore further:

Your initial thoughts:

One of the day's challenges, big or small:

Things you are grateful for today:

Two events or news stories out in the world that caught your attention:

DAILY

POWER UP! (POWER HOUR)

TASK LIST

☐

☐

☐

☐

NOTES AND IDEAS
Fill Out In the Morning

PRAYERS

TODAY'S PRIORITIES
What will make today a win for you?

1)

2)

3)

DAILY REFLECTIONS

THIS MORNING I AM THANKFUL FOR...

1.

2.

3.

10 MINUTES TO
REFLECT ON YOUR DAY

Date:

Three moments you'd like to remember:

One idea from today that you'd like to explore further:

Your initial thoughts:

One of the day's challenges, big or small:

_____
_____
_____

Things you are grateful for today:

_____
_____
_____
_____

Two events or news stories out in the world that caught your attention:

_____
_____

POWER UP! (POWER HOUR)

TASK LIST

☐

☐

☐

☐

NOTES AND IDEAS
Fill Out In the Morning

PRAYERS

TODAY'S PRIORITIES
What will make today a win for you?

1)

2)

3)

DAILY REFLECTIONS

THIS MORNING I AM THANKFUL FOR...

1.

2.

3.

10 MINUTES TO
REFLECT ON YOUR DAY

Date:

Three moments you'd like to remember:

One idea from today that you'd like to explore further:

Your initial thoughts:

One of the day's challenges, big or small:

Things you are grateful for today:

Two events or news stories out in the world that caught your attention:

DAILY

POWER UP! (POWER HOUR)

TASK LIST

☐

☐

☐

☐

NOTES AND IDEAS
Fill Out In the Morning

PRAYERS

TODAY'S PRIORITIES
What will make today a win for you?

1)

2)

3)

DAILY REFLECTIONS

THIS MORNING I AM THANKFUL FOR...

1.

2.

3.

10 MINUTES TO
REFLECT ON YOUR DAY

Date:

Three moments you'd like to remember:

One idea from today that you'd like to explore further:

Your initial thoughts:

One of the day's challenges, big or small:

Things you are grateful for today:

Two events or news stories out in the world that caught your attention:

201

POWER UP! (POWER HOUR)

TASK LIST

☐

☐

☐

☐

NOTES AND IDEAS
Fill Out In the Morning

PRAYERS

TODAY'S PRIORITIES
What will make today a win for you?

1)

2)

3)

DAILY REFLECTIONS

THIS MORNING I AM THANKFUL FOR...

1.

2.

3.

10 MINUTES TO
REFLECT ON YOUR DAY

Date:

Three moments you'd like to remember:

One idea from today that you'd like to explore further:

Your initial thoughts:

One of the day's challenges, big or small:

Things you are grateful for today:

Two events or news stories out in the world that caught your attention:

DAILY

POWER UP! (POWER HOUR)

TASK LIST

☐

☐

☐

☐

NOTES AND IDEAS
Fill Out In the Morning

PRAYERS

TODAY'S PRIORITIES
What will make today a win for you?

1)

2)

3)

DAILY REFLECTIONS

THIS MORNING I AM THANKFUL FOR...

1.

2.

3.

10 MINUTES TO
REFLECT ON YOUR DAY

Date:

Three moments you'd like to remember:

One idea from today that you'd like to explore further:

Your initial thoughts:

One of the day's challenges, big or small:

Two events or news stories out in the world that caught your attention:

Things you are grateful for today:

POWER UP! (POWER HOUR)

TASK LIST

☐

☐

☐

☐

NOTES AND IDEAS
Fill Out In the Morning

PRAYERS

TODAY'S PRIORITIES
What will make today a win for you?

1)

2)

3)

DAILY REFLECTIONS

THIS MORNING I AM THANKFUL FOR...

1.

2.

3.

10 MINUTES TO
REFLECT ON YOUR DAY

Date:

Three moments you'd like to remember:

One idea from today that you'd like to explore further:

Your initial thoughts:

One of the day's challenges, big or small:

Things you are grateful for today:

Two events or news stories out in the world that caught your attention:

207

POWER UP! (POWER HOUR)

TASK LIST

☐

☐

☐

☐

NOTES AND IDEAS
Fill Out In the Morning

PRAYERS

TODAY'S PRIORITIES
What will make today a win for you?

1)

2)

3)

DAILY REFLECTIONS

THIS MORNING I AM THANKFUL FOR...

1.

2.

3.

10 MINUTES TO
REFLECT ON YOUR DAY

Date:

Three moments you'd like to remember:

One idea from today that you'd like to explore further:

Your initial thoughts:

One of the day's challenges, big or small:

_____

_____

_____

Things you are grateful for today:

_____

_____

_____

_____

_____

Two events or news stories out in the world that caught your attention:

_____

_____

209

POWER UP! (POWER HOUR)

TASK LIST

☐

☐

☐

☐

NOTES AND IDEAS
Fill Out In the Morning

PRAYERS

TODAY'S PRIORITIES
What will make today a win for you?

1)

2)

3)

DAILY REFLECTIONS

THIS MORNING I AM THANKFUL FOR...
1.
2.
3.

10 MINUTES TO
REFLECT ON YOUR DAY

Date:

Three moments you'd like to remember:

One idea from today that you'd like to explore further:

Your initial thoughts:

One of the day's challenges, big or small:

Things you are grateful for today:

Two events or news stories out in the world that caught your attention:

DAILY

POWER UP! (POWER HOUR)

TASK LIST

☐

☐

☐

☐

NOTES AND IDEAS
Fill Out In the Morning

PRAYERS

TODAY'S PRIORITIES
What will make today a win for you?

1)

2)

3)

DAILY REFLECTIONS

THIS MORNING I AM THANKFUL FOR...

1.

2.

3.

10 MINUTES TO
REFLECT ON YOUR DAY

Date:

Three moments you'd like to remember:

One idea from today that you'd like to explore further:

Your initial thoughts:

One of the day's challenges, big or small:

_____
_____
_____

Things you are grateful for today:

_____
_____
_____
_____
_____

Two events or news stories out in the world that caught your attention:

_____
_____

POWER UP! (POWER HOUR)

TASK LIST

- [ ]
- [ ]
- [ ]
- [ ]

NOTES AND IDEAS
Fill Out In the Morning

PRAYERS

TODAY'S PRIORITIES
What will make today a win for you?

1)

2)

3)

DAILY REFLECTIONS

THIS MORNING I AM THANKFUL FOR...

1.

2.

3.

10 MINUTES TO
REFLECT ON YOUR DAY

Date:

Three moments you'd like to remember:

One idea from today that you'd like to explore further:

Your initial thoughts:

One of the day's challenges, big or small:

_____
_____
_____

Things you are grateful for today:

_____
_____
_____
_____

Two events or news stories out in the world that caught your attention:

_____
_____

DAILY

POWER UP! (POWER HOUR)

TASK LIST

☐

☐

☐

☐

NOTES AND IDEAS
Fill Out In the Morning

PRAYERS

TODAY'S PRIORITIES
What will make today a win for you?

1)

2)

3)

DAILY REFLECTIONS

THIS MORNING I AM THANKFUL FOR...

1.

2.

3.

10 MINUTES TO
REFLECT ON YOUR DAY

Date:

Three moments you'd like to remember:

One idea from today that you'd like to explore further:

Your initial thoughts:

One of the day's challenges, big or small:

Things you are grateful for today:

Two events or news stories out in the world that caught your attention:

POWER UP! (POWER HOUR)

TASK LIST

☐

☐

☐

☐

NOTES AND IDEAS
Fill Out In the Morning

PRAYERS

TODAY'S PRIORITIES
What will make today a win for you?

1)

2)

3)

DAILY REFLECTIONS

THIS MORNING I AM THANKFUL FOR...

1.

2.

3.

10 MINUTES TO
REFLECT ON YOUR DAY

Date:

Three moments you'd like to remember:

One idea from today that you'd like to explore further:

Your initial thoughts:

One of the day's challenges, big or small:

_____
_____
_____

Things you are grateful for today:

_____
_____
_____

Two events or news stories out in the world that caught your attention:

_____
_____

_____
_____
_____

219

POWER UP! (POWER HOUR)

TASK LIST

☐

☐

☐

☐

NOTES AND IDEAS
Fill Out In the Morning

PRAYERS

TODAY'S PRIORITIES
What will make today a win for you?

1)

2)

3)

DAILY REFLECTIONS

THIS MORNING I AM THANKFUL FOR...

1.

2.

3.

10 MINUTES TO
REFLECT ON YOUR DAY

Date:

Three moments you'd like to remember:

One idea from today that you'd like to explore further:

Your initial thoughts:

One of the day's challenges, big or small:

_____

_____

_____

Things you are grateful for today:

_____

_____

_____

_____

_____

Two events or news stories out in the world that caught your attention:

_____

_____

221

POWER UP! (POWER HOUR)

TASK LIST

- [ ]
- [ ]
- [ ]
- [ ]

NOTES AND IDEAS
Fill Out In the Morning

PRAYERS

TODAY'S PRIORITIES
What will make today a win for you?

1)

2)

3)

DAILY REFLECTIONS

THIS MORNING I AM THANKFUL FOR...

1.

2.

3.

10 MINUTES TO
REFLECT ON YOUR DAY

Date:

Three moments you'd like to remember:

One idea from today that you'd like to explore further:

One of the day's challenges, big or small:

Your initial thoughts:

Things you are grateful for today:

Two events or news stories out in the world that caught your attention:

POWER UP! (POWER HOUR)

TASK LIST

☐

☐

☐

☐

NOTES AND IDEAS
Fill Out In the Morning

PRAYERS

TODAY'S PRIORITIES
What will make today a win for you?

1)

2)

3)

DAILY REFLECTIONS

THIS MORNING I AM THANKFUL FOR...

1.

2.

3.

10 MINUTES TO
REFLECT ON YOUR DAY

Date:

Three moments you'd like to remember:

One idea from today that you'd like to explore further:

Your initial thoughts:

One of the day's challenges, big or small:

Things you are grateful for today:

Two events or news stories out in the world that caught your attention:

POWER UP! (POWER HOUR)

TASK LIST

☐

☐

☐

☐

NOTES AND IDEAS
Fill Out In the Morning

PRAYERS

TODAY'S PRIORITIES
What will make today a win for you?

1)

2)

3)

DAILY REFLECTIONS

THIS MORNING I AM THANKFUL FOR...

1.

2.

3.

10 MINUTES TO
REFLECT ON YOUR DAY

Date:

Three moments you'd like to remember:

One idea from today that you'd like to explore further:

One of the day's challenges, big or small:

Your initial thoughts:

Things you are grateful for today:

Two events or news stories out in the world that caught your attention:

POWER UP! (POWER HOUR)

TASK LIST

☐

☐

☐

☐

NOTES AND IDEAS
Fill Out In the Morning

PRAYERS

TODAY'S PRIORITIES
What will make today a win for you?

1)

2)

3)

DAILY REFLECTIONS

THIS MORNING I AM THANKFUL FOR...

1.

2.

3.

10 MINUTES TO
REFLECT ON YOUR DAY

Date:

Three moments you'd like to remember:

One idea from today that you'd like to explore further:

Your initial thoughts:

One of the day's challenges, big or small:

Things you are grateful for today:

Two events or news stories out in the world that caught your attention:

229

POWER UP! (POWER HOUR)

TASK LIST

☐

☐

☐

☐

NOTES AND IDEAS
Fill Out In the Morning

PRAYERS

TODAY'S PRIORITIES
What will make today a win for you?

1)

2)

3)

DAILY REFLECTIONS

THIS MORNING I AM THANKFUL FOR...

1.

2.

3.

10 MINUTES TO
REFLECT ON YOUR DAY

Date:

Three moments you'd like to remember:

One idea from today that you'd like to explore further:

One of the day's challenges, big or small:

Your initial thoughts:

Things you are grateful for today:

Two events or news stories out in the world that caught your attention:

DAILY

POWER UP! (POWER HOUR)

TASK LIST

☐

☐

☐

☐

NOTES AND IDEAS
Fill Out In the Morning

PRAYERS

TODAY'S PRIORITIES
What will make today a win for you?

1)

2)

3)

DAILY REFLECTIONS

THIS MORNING I AM THANKFUL FOR...

1.

2.

3.

10 MINUTES TO
REFLECT ON YOUR DAY

Date:

Three moments you'd like to remember:

One idea from today that you'd like to explore further:

Your initial thoughts:

One of the day's challenges, big or small:

Things you are grateful for today:

Two events or news stories out in the world that caught your attention:

POWER UP! (POWER HOUR)

TASK LIST

☐

☐

☐

☐

NOTES AND IDEAS
Fill Out In the Morning

PRAYERS

TODAY'S PRIORITIES
What will make today a win for you?

1)

2)

3)

DAILY REFLECTIONS

THIS MORNING I AM THANKFUL FOR...

1.

2.

3.

234

10 MINUTES TO
REFLECT ON YOUR DAY

Date:

Three moments you'd like to remember:

One idea from today that you'd like to explore further:

One of the day's challenges, big or small:

Your initial thoughts:

Things you are grateful for today:

Two events or news stories out in the world that caught your attention:

DAILY

POWER UP! (POWER HOUR)

TASK LIST

- ☐
- ☐
- ☐
- ☐

NOTES AND IDEAS
Fill Out In the Morning

PRAYERS

TODAY'S PRIORITIES
What will make today a win for you?

1)

2)

3)

DAILY REFLECTIONS

THIS MORNING I AM THANKFUL FOR...

1.
2.
3.

10 MINUTES TO
REFLECT ON YOUR DAY

Date:

Three moments you'd like to remember:

One idea from today that you'd like to explore further:

Your initial thoughts:

One of the day's challenges, big or small:

Things you are grateful for today:

Two events or news stories out in the world that caught your attention:

237

POWER UP! (POWER HOUR)

TASK LIST

- [ ]
- [ ]
- [ ]
- [ ]

NOTES AND IDEAS
Fill Out In the Morning

PRAYERS

TODAY'S PRIORITIES
What will make today a win for you?

1)

2)

3)

DAILY REFLECTIONS

THIS MORNING I AM THANKFUL FOR...

1.

2.

3.

10 MINUTES TO
REFLECT ON YOUR DAY

Date:

Three moments you'd like to remember:

One idea from today that you'd like to explore further:

One of the day's challenges, big or small:

Your initial thoughts:

Things you are grateful for today:

Two events or news stories out in the world that caught your attention:

POWER HOUR WORKSHEET

POWER UP! (POWER HOUR)

TASK LIST

☐

☐

☐

☐

NOTES AND IDEAS
Fill Out In the Morning

PRAYERS

TODAY'S PRIORITIES
What will make today a win for you?

1)

2)

3)

DAILY REFLECTIONS

THIS MORNING I AM THANKFUL FOR...

1.

2.

3.

10 MINUTES TO
REFLECT ON YOUR DAY

Date:

Three moments you'd like to remember:

One idea from today that you'd like to explore further:

Your initial thoughts:

One of the day's challenges, big or small:

_____

_____

_____

Things you are grateful for today:

_____

_____

_____

_____

_____

Two events or news stories out in the world that caught your attention:

_____

_____

241

POWER UP! (POWER HOUR)

TASK LIST

☐

☐

☐

☐

NOTES AND IDEAS
Fill Out In the Morning

PRAYERS

TODAY'S PRIORITIES
What will make today a win for you?

1)

2)

3)

DAILY REFLECTIONS

THIS MORNING I AM THANKFUL FOR...

1.

2.

3.

10 MINUTES TO
REFLECT ON YOUR DAY

Date:

Three moments you'd like to remember:

One idea from today that you'd like to explore further:

Your initial thoughts:

One of the day's challenges, big or small:

_____

_____

_____

Things you are grateful for today:

_____

_____

_____

Two events or news stories out in the world that caught your attention:

_____

_____

_____

_____

243

DAILY

POWER UP! (POWER HOUR)

TASK LIST

☐

☐

☐

☐

NOTES AND IDEAS
Fill Out In the Morning

PRAYERS

TODAY'S PRIORITIES
What will make today a win for you?

1)

2)

3)

DAILY REFLECTIONS

THIS MORNING I AM THANKFUL FOR...

1.

2.

3.

10 MINUTES TO
REFLECT ON YOUR DAY

Date:

Three moments you'd like to remember:

One idea from today that you'd like to explore further:

Your initial thoughts:

One of the day's challenges, big or small:

Things you are grateful for today:

Two events or news stories out in the world that caught your attention:

POWER UP! (POWER HOUR)

TASK LIST

☐

☐

☐

☐

NOTES AND IDEAS
Fill Out In the Morning

PRAYERS

TODAY'S PRIORITIES
What will make today a win for you?

1)

2)

3)

DAILY REFLECTIONS

THIS MORNING I AM THANKFUL FOR...

1.

2.

3.

10 MINUTES TO
REFLECT ON YOUR DAY

Date:

Three moments you'd like to remember:

One idea from today that you'd like to explore further:

Your initial thoughts:

One of the day's challenges, big or small:

Things you are grateful for today:

Two events or news stories out in the world that caught your attention:

DAILY

POWER UP! (POWER HOUR)

TASK LIST

☐

☐

☐

☐

NOTES AND IDEAS
Fill Out In the Morning

PRAYERS

TODAY'S PRIORITIES
What will make today a win for you?

1)

2)

3)

DAILY REFLECTIONS

THIS MORNING I AM THANKFUL FOR...

1.

2.

3.

10 MINUTES TO
REFLECT ON YOUR DAY

Date:

Three moments you'd like to remember:

One idea from today that you'd like to explore further:

Your initial thoughts:

One of the day's challenges, big or small:

_____

_____

_____

Things you are grateful for today:

_____

_____

_____

_____

_____

Two events or news stories out in the world that caught your attention:

_____

_____

249

POWER UP! (POWER HOUR)

TASK LIST

☐

☐

☐

☐

NOTES AND IDEAS
Fill Out In the Morning

PRAYERS

TODAY'S PRIORITIES
What will make today a win for you?

1)

2)

3)

DAILY REFLECTIONS

THIS MORNING I AM THANKFUL FOR...

1.

2.

3.

10 MINUTES TO
REFLECT ON YOUR DAY

Date:

Three moments you'd like to remember:

One idea from today that you'd like to explore further:

One of the day's challenges, big or small:

Your initial thoughts:

Things you are grateful for today:

Two events or news stories out in the world that caught your attention:

POWER UP! (POWER HOUR)

TASK LIST

☐

☐

☐

☐

NOTES AND IDEAS
Fill Out In the Morning

PRAYERS

TODAY'S PRIORITIES
What will make today a win for you?

1)

2)

3)

DAILY REFLECTIONS

THIS MORNING I AM THANKFUL FOR...

1.

2.

3.

10 MINUTES TO
REFLECT ON YOUR DAY

Date:

Three moments you'd like to remember:

One idea from today that you'd like to explore further:

Your initial thoughts:

One of the day's challenges, big or small:

Things you are grateful for today:

Two events or news stories out in the world that caught your attention:

POWER UP! (POWER HOUR)

TASK LIST

☐

☐

☐

☐

NOTES AND IDEAS
Fill Out In the Morning

PRAYERS

TODAY'S PRIORITIES
What will make today a win for you?

1)

2)

3)

DAILY REFLECTIONS

THIS MORNING I AM THANKFUL FOR...

1.

2.

3.

10 MINUTES TO
REFLECT ON YOUR DAY

Date:

Three moments you'd like to remember:

One idea from today that you'd like to explore further:

Your initial thoughts:

Two events or news stories out in the world that caught your attention:

One of the day's challenges, big or small:

Things you are grateful for today:

255

DAILY

POWER UP! (POWER HOUR)

TASK LIST

☐

☐

☐

☐

NOTES AND IDEAS
Fill Out In the Morning

PRAYERS

TODAY'S PRIORITIES
What will make today a win for you?

1)

2)

3)

DAILY REFLECTIONS

THIS MORNING I AM THANKFUL FOR...

1.

2.

3.

10 MINUTES TO
REFLECT ON YOUR DAY

Date:

Three moments you'd like to remember:

One idea from today that you'd like to explore further:

Your initial thoughts:

One of the day's challenges, big or small:

Things you are grateful for today:

Two events or news stories out in the world that caught your attention:

DAILY

POWER UP! (POWER HOUR)

TASK LIST

☐

☐

☐

☐

NOTES AND IDEAS
Fill Out In the Morning

PRAYERS

TODAY'S PRIORITIES
What will make today a win for you?

1)

2)

3)

DAILY REFLECTIONS

THIS MORNING I AM THANKFUL FOR...

1.

2.

3.

10 MINUTES TO
REFLECT ON YOUR DAY

Date:

Three moments you'd like to remember:

One idea from today that you'd like to explore further:

Your initial thoughts:

One of the day's challenges, big or small:

_____

_____

_____

Things you are grateful for today:

_____

_____

_____

_____

Two events or news stories out in the world that caught your attention:

_____

_____

POWER UP! (POWER HOUR)

TASK LIST

☐

☐

☐

☐

NOTES AND IDEAS
Fill Out In the Morning

PRAYERS

TODAY'S PRIORITIES
What will make today a win for you?

1)

2)

3)

DAILY REFLECTIONS

THIS MORNING I AM THANKFUL FOR...

1.

2.

3.

10 MINUTES TO
REFLECT ON YOUR DAY

Date:

Three moments you'd like to remember:

One idea from today that you'd like to explore further:

Your initial thoughts:

Two events or news stories out in the world that caught your attention:

One of the day's challenges, big or small:

Things you are grateful for today:

POWER UP! (POWER HOUR)

TASK LIST

☐

☐

☐

☐

NOTES AND IDEAS
Fill Out In the Morning

PRAYERS

TODAY'S PRIORITIES
What will make today a win for you?

1)

2)

3)

DAILY REFLECTIONS

THIS MORNING I AM THANKFUL FOR...

1.

2.

3.

10 MINUTES TO
REFLECT ON YOUR DAY

Date:

Three moments you'd like to remember:

One idea from today that you'd like to explore further:

Your initial thoughts:

One of the day's challenges, big or small:

Things you are grateful for today:

Two events or news stories out in the world that caught your attention:

DAILY

POWER UP! (POWER HOUR)

TASK LIST

- [ ]
- [ ]
- [ ]
- [ ]

NOTES AND IDEAS
Fill Out In the Morning

PRAYERS

TODAY'S PRIORITIES
What will make today a win for you?

1)

2)

3)

DAILY REFLECTIONS

THIS MORNING I AM THANKFUL FOR...

1.

2.

3.

10 MINUTES TO
REFLECT ON YOUR DAY

Date:

Three moments you'd like to remember:

One idea from today that you'd like to explore further:

Your initial thoughts:

One of the day's challenges, big or small:

Things you are grateful for today:

Two events or news stories out in the world that caught your attention:

DAILY

POWER UP! (POWER HOUR)

TASK LIST

☐

☐

☐

☐

NOTES AND IDEAS
Fill Out In the Morning

PRAYERS

TODAY'S PRIORITIES
What will make today a win for you?

1)

2)

3)

DAILY REFLECTIONS

THIS MORNING I AM THANKFUL FOR...

1.

2.

3.

10 MINUTES TO
REFLECT ON YOUR DAY

Date:

Three moments you'd like to remember:

One idea from today that you'd like to explore further:

Your initial thoughts:

One of the day's challenges, big or small:

_____
_____
_____

Things you are grateful for today:

_____
_____
_____
_____
_____

Two events or news stories out in the world that caught your attention:

_____
_____

267

DAILY

POWER UP! (POWER HOUR)

TASK LIST

☐

☐

☐

☐

NOTES AND IDEAS
Fill Out In the Morning

PRAYERS

TODAY'S PRIORITIES
What will make today a win for you?

1)

2)

3)

DAILY REFLECTIONS

THIS MORNING I AM THANKFUL FOR...

1.

2.

3.

10 MINUTES TO
REFLECT ON YOUR DAY

Date:

Three moments you'd like to remember:

One idea from today that you'd like to explore further:

Your initial thoughts:

One of the day's challenges, big or small:

Things you are grateful for today:

Two events or news stories out in the world that caught your attention:

POWER UP! (POWER HOUR)

TASK LIST

☐

☐

☐

☐

NOTES AND IDEAS
Fill Out In the Morning

PRAYERS

TODAY'S PRIORITIES
What will make today a win for you?

1)

2)

3)

DAILY REFLECTIONS

THIS MORNING I AM THANKFUL FOR...

1.

2.

3.

10 MINUTES TO
REFLECT ON YOUR DAY

Date:

Three moments you'd like to remember:

One idea from today that you'd like to explore further:

Your initial thoughts:

One of the day's challenges, big or small:

_____

_____

_____

Things you are grateful for today:

_____

_____

_____

_____

Two events or news stories out in the world that caught your attention:

_____

_____

271

POWER UP! (POWER HOUR)

TASK LIST

☐

☐

☐

☐

NOTES AND IDEAS
Fill Out In the Morning

PRAYERS

TODAY'S PRIORITIES
What will make today a win for you?

1)

2)

3)

DAILY REFLECTIONS

THIS MORNING I AM THANKFUL FOR...

1.

2.

3.

10 MINUTES TO
REFLECT ON YOUR DAY

Date:

Three moments you'd like to remember:

One idea from today that you'd like to explore further:

Your initial thoughts:

One of the day's challenges, big or small:

_____
_____
_____

Things you are grateful for today:

_____
_____
_____
_____

Two events or news stories out in the world that caught your attention:

_____
_____

273

POWER UP! (POWER HOUR)

TASK LIST

☐

☐

☐

☐

NOTES AND IDEAS
Fill Out In the Morning

PRAYERS

TODAY'S PRIORITIES
What will make today a win for you?

1)

2)

3)

DAILY REFLECTIONS

THIS MORNING I AM THANKFUL FOR...

1.

2.

3.

10 MINUTES TO
REFLECT ON YOUR DAY

Date:

Three moments you'd like to remember:

One idea from today that you'd like to explore further:

Your initial thoughts:

One of the day's challenges, big or small:

_____

_____

_____

Things you are grateful for today:

_____

_____

_____

_____

_____

_____

Two events or news stories out in the world that caught your attention:

_____

_____

DAILY

POWER UP! (POWER HOUR)

TASK LIST

- [ ]
- [ ]
- [ ]
- [ ]

NOTES AND IDEAS
Fill Out In the Morning

PRAYERS

TODAY'S PRIORITIES
What will make today a win for you?

1)

2)

3)

DAILY REFLECTIONS

THIS MORNING I AM THANKFUL FOR...

1.

2.

3.

10 MINUTES TO
REFLECT ON YOUR DAY

Date:

Three moments you'd like to remember:

One idea from today that you'd like to explore further:

Your initial thoughts:

One of the day's challenges, big or small:

Things you are grateful for today:

Two events or news stories out in the world that caught your attention:

10 MINUTES TO
REFLECT ON YOUR DAY

Date:

Three moments you'd like to remember:

One idea from today that you'd like to explore further:

Your initial thoughts:

One of the day's challenges, big or small:

_____
_____
_____

Things you are grateful for today:

_____
_____
_____
_____
_____

Two events or news stories out in the world that caught your attention:

_____
_____

DAILY

POWER UP! (POWER HOUR)

TASK LIST

☐

☐

☐

☐

NOTES AND IDEAS
Fill Out In the Morning

PRAYERS

TODAY'S PRIORITIES
What will make today a win for you?

1)

2)

3)

DAILY REFLECTIONS

THIS MORNING I AM THANKFUL FOR...

1.

2.

3.

10 MINUTES TO
REFLECT ON YOUR DAY

Date:

Three moments you'd like to remember:

One idea from today that you'd like to explore further:

Your initial thoughts:

One of the day's challenges, big or small:

_____
_____
_____

Things you are grateful for today:

_____
_____
_____
_____

Two events or news stories out in the world that caught your attention:

_____
_____

_____
_____

POWER UP! (POWER HOUR)

TASK LIST

☐

☐

☐

☐

NOTES AND IDEAS
Fill Out In the Morning

PRAYERS

TODAY'S PRIORITIES
What will make today a win for you?

1)

2)

3)

DAILY REFLECTIONS

THIS MORNING I AM THANKFUL FOR...

1.

2.

3.

10 MINUTES TO
REFLECT ON YOUR DAY

Date:

Three moments you'd like to remember:

One idea from today that you'd like to explore further:

Your initial thoughts:

One of the day's challenges, big or small:

_____

_____

_____

Things you are grateful for today:

_____

_____

_____

_____

_____

Two events or news stories out in the world that caught your attention:

_____

_____

283

DAILY

POWER UP! (POWER HOUR)

TASK LIST

☐

☐

☐

☐

NOTES AND IDEAS
Fill Out In the Morning

PRAYERS

TODAY'S PRIORITIES
What will make today a win for you?

1)

2)

3)

DAILY REFLECTIONS

THIS MORNING I AM THANKFUL FOR...

1.

2.

3.

10 MINUTES TO
REFLECT ON YOUR DAY

Date:

Three moments you'd like to remember:

One idea from today that you'd like to explore further:

Your initial thoughts:

Two events or news stories out in the world that caught your attention:

One of the day's challenges, big or small:

Things you are grateful for today:

DAILY

POWER UP! (POWER HOUR)

TASK LIST

☐

☐

☐

☐

NOTES AND IDEAS
Fill Out In the Morning

PRAYERS

TODAY'S PRIORITIES
What will make today a win for you?

1)

2)

3)

DAILY REFLECTIONS

THIS MORNING I AM THANKFUL FOR...

1.

2.

3.

10 MINUTES TO
REFLECT ON YOUR DAY

Date:

Three moments you'd like to remember:

One idea from today that you'd like to explore further:

Your initial thoughts:

One of the day's challenges, big or small:

Things you are grateful for today:

Two events or news stories out in the world that caught your attention:

POWER UP! (POWER HOUR)

TASK LIST

☐

☐

☐

☐

NOTES AND IDEAS
Fill Out In the Morning

PRAYERS

TODAY'S PRIORITIES
What will make today a win for you?

1)

2)

3)

DAILY REFLECTIONS

THIS MORNING I AM THANKFUL FOR...

1.

2.

3.

10 MINUTES TO
REFLECT ON YOUR DAY

Date:

Three moments you'd like to remember:

One idea from today that you'd like to explore further:

Your initial thoughts:

One of the day's challenges, big or small:

_____

_____

_____

Things you are grateful for today:

_____

_____

_____

_____

_____

Two events or news stories out in the world that caught your attention:

_____

_____

POWER UP! (POWER HOUR)

TASK LIST

☐

☐

☐

☐

NOTES AND IDEAS
Fill Out In the Morning

PRAYERS

TODAY'S PRIORITIES
What will make today a win for you?

1)

2)

3)

DAILY REFLECTIONS

THIS MORNING I AM THANKFUL FOR...

1.

2.

3.

10 MINUTES TO
REFLECT ON YOUR DAY

Date:

Three moments you'd like to remember:

One idea from today that you'd like to explore further:

Your initial thoughts:

One of the day's challenges, big or small:

Things you are grateful for today:

Two events or news stories out in the world that caught your attention:

POWER UP! (POWER HOUR)

TASK LIST

☐

☐

☐

☐

NOTES AND IDEAS
Fill Out In the Morning

PRAYERS

TODAY'S PRIORITIES
What will make today a win for you?

1)

2)

3)

DAILY REFLECTIONS

THIS MORNING I AM THANKFUL FOR...

1.

2.

3.

10 MINUTES TO
REFLECT ON YOUR DAY

Date:

Three moments you'd like to remember:

One idea from today that you'd like to explore further:

Your initial thoughts:

One of the day's challenges, big or small:

_____

_____

_____

Things you are grateful for today:

_____

_____

_____

Two events or news stories out in the world that caught your attention:

_____

_____

_____

_____

293

WORKSHEET:
PEAK PERFORMANCE

Do this worksheet every week

I adapted this form from *New York Times* best-selling author Darren Hardy. We both recommend that you fill it in once a week, with an accountability partner. Darren suggests that you choose someone from an entirely different business and meet weekly over coffee, but I choose to do this worksheet with Shaun Chiodo, my partner in our salon coaching business and the COO of my companies, and it works well for us.

Peak Performance Weekly Questions:

1. Most Important: Weekly focuses

2. Wins: 1–3 major accomplishments of the week

3. Losses: 1–3 areas of commitments you failed on

4. Fixes: What will you do next week to ensure it doesn't happen again?

5. Ahas: Greatest learning experiences throughout the week

6. Solicit needed feedback: To hold each other accountable

Peak Performance Weekly Questions

Month _____ Week _____

1. Most Important: Weekly focuses

2. Wins: 1–3 major accomplishments of the week

3. Losses: 1–3 areas of commitments you failed on

4. Fixes: What will you do next week to ensure it doesn't happen again?

5. Ahas: Greatest learning experiences throughout the week

6. Solicit needed feedback: To hold each other accountable

Peak Performance Weekly Questions

Month _____   Week _____

1. Most Important: Weekly focuses

2. Wins: 1–3 major accomplishments of the week

3. Losses: 1–3 areas of commitments you failed on

4. Fixes: What will you do next week to ensure it doesn't happen again?

5. Ahas: Greatest learning experiences throughout the week

6. Solicit needed feedback: To hold each other accountable

Peak Performance Weekly Questions

Month _____ Week _____

1. **Most Important:** Weekly focuses

2. **Wins:** 1–3 major accomplishments of the week

3. **Losses:** 1–3 areas of commitments you failed on

4. **Fixes:** What will you do next week to ensure it doesn't happen again?

5. **Ahas:** Greatest learning experiences throughout the week

6. **Solicit needed feedback:** To hold each other accountable

Peak Performance Weekly Questions

Month _____   Week _____

1. Most Important: Weekly focuses

2. Wins: 1–3 major accomplishments of the week

3. Losses: 1–3 areas of commitments you failed on

4. Fixes: What will you do next week to ensure it doesn't happen again?

5. Ahas: Greatest learning experiences throughout the week

6. Solicit needed feedback: To hold each other accountable

Peak Performance Weekly Questions

Month _____ Week _____

1. Most Important: Weekly focuses

2. Wins: 1–3 major accomplishments of the week

3. Losses: 1–3 areas of commitments you failed on

4. Fixes: What will you do next week to ensure it doesn't happen again?

5. Ahas: Greatest learning experiences throughout the week

6. Solicit needed feedback: To hold each other accountable

Peak Performance Weekly Questions

Month _____   Week _____

1. Most Important: Weekly focuses

2. Wins: 1–3 major accomplishments of the week

3. Losses: 1–3 areas of commitments you failed on

4. Fixes: What will you do next week to ensure it doesn't happen again?

5. Ahas: Greatest learning experiences throughout the week

6. Solicit needed feedback: To hold each other accountable

Peak Performance Weekly Questions

Month _____ Week _____

1. Most Important: Weekly focuses

2. Wins: 1–3 major accomplishments of the week

3. Losses: 1–3 areas of commitments you failed on

4. Fixes: What will you do next week to ensure it doesn't happen again?

5. Ahas: Greatest learning experiences throughout the week

6. Solicit needed feedback: To hold each other accountable

Peak Performance Weekly Questions

Month _____ Week _____

1. Most Important: Weekly focuses

2. Wins: 1–3 major accomplishments of the week

3. Losses: 1–3 areas of commitments you failed on

4. Fixes: What will you do next week to ensure it doesn't happen again?

5. Ahas: Greatest learning experiences throughout the week

6. Solicit needed feedback: To hold each other accountable

Peak Performance Weekly Questions

Month _____ Week _____

1. Most Important: Weekly focuses

2. Wins: 1–3 major accomplishments of the week

3. Losses: 1–3 areas of commitments you failed on

4. Fixes: What will you do next week to ensure it doesn't happen again?

5. Ahas: Greatest learning experiences throughout the week

6. Solicit needed feedback: To hold each other accountable

Peak Performance Weekly Questions

Month _____ Week _____

1. Most Important: Weekly focuses

2. Wins: 1–3 major accomplishments of the week

3. Losses: 1–3 areas of commitments you failed on

4. Fixes: What will you do next week to ensure it doesn't happen again?

5. Ahas: Greatest learning experiences throughout the week

6. Solicit needed feedback: To hold each other accountable

Peak Performance Weekly Questions

Month _____ Week _____

1. Most Important: Weekly focuses

2. Wins: 1–3 major accomplishments of the week

3. Losses: 1–3 areas of commitments you failed on

4. Fixes: What will you do next week to ensure it doesn't happen again?

5. Ahas: Greatest learning experiences throughout the week

6. Solicit needed feedback: To hold each other accountable

Peak Performance Weekly Questions

Month _____   Week _____

1. Most Important: Weekly focuses

2. Wins: 1–3 major accomplishments of the week

3. Losses: 1–3 areas of commitments you failed on

4. Fixes: What will you do next week to ensure it doesn't happen again?

5. Ahas: Greatest learning experiences throughout the week

6. Solicit needed feedback: To hold each other accountable

Peak Performance Weekly Questions

Month _____ Week _____

WEEKLY

1. Most Important: Weekly focuses

2. Wins: 1–3 major accomplishments of the week

3. Losses: 1–3 areas of commitments you failed on

4. Fixes: What will you do next week to ensure it doesn't happen again?

5. Ahas: Greatest learning experiences throughout the week

6. Solicit needed feedback: To hold each other accountable

Peak Performance Weekly Questions

Month _____ Week _____

1. Most Important: Weekly focuses

2. Wins: 1–3 major accomplishments of the week

3. Losses: 1–3 areas of commitments you failed on

4. Fixes: What will you do next week to ensure it doesn't happen again?

5. Ahas: Greatest learning experiences throughout the week

6. Solicit needed feedback: To hold each other accountable

Peak Performance Weekly Questions

Month _____ Week _____

1. Most Important: Weekly focuses

2. Wins: 1–3 major accomplishments of the week

3. Losses: 1–3 areas of commitments you failed on

4. Fixes: What will you do next week to ensure it doesn't happen again?

5. Ahas: Greatest learning experiences throughout the week

6. Solicit needed feedback: To hold each other accountable

Peak Performance Weekly Questions

Month _____   Week _____

1. Most Important: Weekly focuses

2. Wins:1–3 major accomplishments of the week

3. Losses:1–3 areas of commitments you failed on

4. Fixes: What will you do next week to ensure it doesn't happen again?

5. Ahas: Greatest learning experiences throughout the week

6. Solicit needed feedback: To hold each other accountable

Peak Performance Weekly Questions

Month _____ Week _____

1. Most Important: Weekly focuses

2. Wins: 1–3 major accomplishments of the week

3. Losses: 1–3 areas of commitments you failed on

4. Fixes: What will you do next week to ensure it doesn't happen again?

5. Ahas: Greatest learning experiences throughout the week

6. Solicit needed feedback: To hold each other accountable

Peak Performance Weekly Questions

Month _____ Week _____

1. Most Important: Weekly focuses

2. Wins: 1–3 major accomplishments of the week

3. Losses: 1–3 areas of commitments you failed on

4. Fixes: What will you do next week to ensure it doesn't happen again?

5. Ahas: Greatest learning experiences throughout the week

6. Solicit needed feedback: To hold each other accountable

Peak Performance Weekly Questions

Month _____   Week _____

1. Most Important: Weekly focuses

2. Wins: 1–3 major accomplishments of the week

3. Losses: 1–3 areas of commitments you failed on

4. Fixes: What will you do next week to ensure it doesn't happen again?

5. Ahas: Greatest learning experiences throughout the week

6. Solicit needed feedback: To hold each other accountable

Peak Performance Weekly Questions

Month _____ Week _____

1. Most Important: Weekly focuses

2. Wins: 1–3 major accomplishments of the week

3. Losses: 1–3 areas of commitments you failed on

4. Fixes: What will you do next week to ensure it doesn't happen again?

5. Ahas: Greatest learning experiences throughout the week

6. Solicit needed feedback: To hold each other accountable

Peak Performance Weekly Questions

Month _____ Week _____

1. Most Important: Weekly focuses

2. Wins: 1–3 major accomplishments of the week

3. Losses: 1–3 areas of commitments you failed on

4. Fixes: What will you do next week to ensure it doesn't happen again?

5. Ahas: Greatest learning experiences throughout the week

6. Solicit needed feedback: To hold each other accountable

Peak Performance Weekly Questions

Month _____ Week _____

1. Most Important: Weekly focuses

2. Wins: 1–3 major accomplishments of the week

3. Losses: 1–3 areas of commitments you failed on

4. Fixes: What will you do next week to ensure it doesn't happen again?

5. Ahas: Greatest learning experiences throughout the week

6. Solicit needed feedback: To hold each other accountable

Peak Performance Weekly Questions

Month _____ Week _____

1. Most Important: Weekly focuses

2. Wins: 1–3 major accomplishments of the week

3. Losses: 1–3 areas of commitments you failed on

4. Fixes: What will you do next week to ensure it doesn't happen again?

5. Ahas: Greatest learning experiences throughout the week

6. Solicit needed feedback: To hold each other accountable

Peak Performance Weekly Questions

Month _____   Week _____

1. Most Important: Weekly focuses

2. Wins:1–3 major accomplishments of the week

3. Losses: 1–3 areas of commitments you failed on

4. Fixes: What will you do next week to ensure it doesn't happen again?

5. Ahas: Greatest learning experiences throughout the week

6. Solicit needed feedback: To hold each other accountable

Peak Performance Weekly Questions

Month _____ Week _____

1. Most Important: Weekly focuses

2. Wins: 1–3 major accomplishments of the week

3. Losses: 1–3 areas of commitments you failed on

4. Fixes: What will you do next week to ensure it doesn't happen again?

5. Ahas: Greatest learning experiences throughout the week

6. Solicit needed feedback: To hold each other accountable

Peak Performance Weekly Questions

Month _____ Week _____

1. Most Important: Weekly focuses

2. Wins: 1–3 major accomplishments of the week

3. Losses: 1–3 areas of commitments you failed on

4. Fixes: What will you do next week to ensure it doesn't happen again?

5. Ahas: Greatest learning experiences throughout the week

6. Solicit needed feedback: To hold each other accountable

Peak Performance Weekly Questions

Month _____ Week _____

1. Most Important: Weekly focuses

2. Wins: 1–3 major accomplishments of the week

3. Losses: 1–3 areas of commitments you failed on

4. Fixes: What will you do next week to ensure it doesn't happen again?

5. Ahas: Greatest learning experiences throughout the week

6. Solicit needed feedback: To hold each other accountable

Peak Performance Weekly Questions

Month _____ Week _____

1. Most Important: Weekly focuses

2. Wins: 1–3 major accomplishments of the week

3. Losses: 1–3 areas of commitments you failed on

4. Fixes: What will you do next week to ensure it doesn't happen again?

5. Ahas: Greatest learning experiences throughout the week

6. Solicit needed feedback: To hold each other accountable

Peak Performance Weekly Questions

Month _____ Week _____

WEEKLY

1. Most Important: Weekly focuses

2. Wins: 1–3 major accomplishments of the week

3. Losses: 1–3 areas of commitments you failed on

4. Fixes: What will you do next week to ensure it doesn't happen again?

5. Ahas: Greatest learning experiences throughout the week

6. Solicit needed feedback: To hold each other accountable

Peak Performance Weekly Questions

Month _____   Week _____

1. Most Important: Weekly focuses

2. Wins: 1–3 major accomplishments of the week

3. Losses: 1–3 areas of commitments you failed on

4. Fixes: What will you do next week to ensure it doesn't happen again?

5. Ahas: Greatest learning experiences throughout the week

6. Solicit needed feedback: To hold each other accountable

Peak Performance Weekly Questions

Month _____ Week _____

1. Most Important: Weekly focuses

2. Wins: 1–3 major accomplishments of the week

3. Losses: 1–3 areas of commitments you failed on

4. Fixes: What will you do next week to ensure it doesn't happen again?

5. Ahas: Greatest learning experiences throughout the week

6. Solicit needed feedback: To hold each other accountable

Peak Performance Weekly Questions

Month _____ Week _____

1. Most Important: Weekly focuses

2. Wins: 1–3 major accomplishments of the week

3. Losses: 1–3 areas of commitments you failed on

4. Fixes: What will you do next week to ensure it doesn't happen again?

5. Ahas: Greatest learning experiences throughout the week

6. Solicit needed feedback: To hold each other accountable

Peak Performance Weekly Questions

Month _____ Week _____

WEEKLY

1. Most Important: Weekly focuses

2. Wins: 1–3 major accomplishments of the week

3. Losses: 1–3 areas of commitments you failed on

4. Fixes: What will you do next week to ensure it doesn't happen again?

5. Ahas: Greatest learning experiences throughout the week

6. Solicit needed feedback: To hold each other accountable

Peak Performance Weekly Questions

Month _____ Week _____

1. Most Important: Weekly focuses

2. Wins: 1–3 major accomplishments of the week

3. Losses: 1–3 areas of commitments you failed on

4. Fixes: What will you do next week to ensure it doesn't happen again?

5. Ahas: Greatest learning experiences throughout the week

6. Solicit needed feedback: To hold each other accountable

Peak Performance Weekly Questions

Month _____ Week _____

1. Most Important: Weekly focuses

2. Wins: 1–3 major accomplishments of the week

3. Losses: 1–3 areas of commitments you failed on

4. Fixes: What will you do next week to ensure it doesn't happen again?

5. Ahas: Greatest learning experiences throughout the week

6. Solicit needed feedback: To hold each other accountable

Peak Performance Weekly Questions

Month _____ Week _____

1. Most Important: Weekly focuses

2. Wins: 1–3 major accomplishments of the week

3. Losses: 1–3 areas of commitments you failed on

4. Fixes: What will you do next week to ensure it doesn't happen again?

5. Ahas: Greatest learning experiences throughout the week

6. Solicit needed feedback: To hold each other accountable

Peak Performance Weekly Questions

Month _____ Week _____

1. Most Important: Weekly focuses

2. Wins: 1–3 major accomplishments of the week

3. Losses: 1–3 areas of commitments you failed on

4. Fixes: What will you do next week to ensure it doesn't happen again?

5. Ahas: Greatest learning experiences throughout the week

6. Solicit needed feedback: To hold each other accountable

Peak Performance Weekly Questions

Month _____ Week _____

1. Most Important: Weekly focuses

2. Wins: 1–3 major accomplishments of the week

3. Losses: 1–3 areas of commitments you failed on

4. Fixes: What will you do next week to ensure it doesn't happen again?

5. Ahas: Greatest learning experiences throughout the week

6. Solicit needed feedback: To hold each other accountable

Peak Performance Weekly Questions

Month _____ Week _____

1. Most Important: Weekly focuses

2. Wins: 1–3 major accomplishments of the week

3. Losses: 1–3 areas of commitments you failed on

4. Fixes: What will you do next week to ensure it doesn't happen again?

5. Ahas: Greatest learning experiences throughout the week

6. Solicit needed feedback: To hold each other accountable

Peak Performance Weekly Questions

Month _____   Week _____

1. Most Important: Weekly focuses

2. Wins: 1–3 major accomplishments of the week

3. Losses: 1–3 areas of commitments you failed on

4. Fixes: What will you do next week to ensure it doesn't happen again?

5. Ahas: Greatest learning experiences throughout the week

6. Solicit needed feedback: To hold each other accountable

Peak Performance Weekly Questions

Month _____ Week _____

1. Most Important: Weekly focuses

2. Wins: 1–3 major accomplishments of the week

3. Losses: 1–3 areas of commitments you failed on

4. Fixes: What will you do next week to ensure it doesn't happen again?

5. Ahas: Greatest learning experiences throughout the week

6. Solicit needed feedback: To hold each other accountable

Peak Performance Weekly Questions

Month _____   Week _____

1. Most Important: Weekly focuses

2. Wins: 1–3 major accomplishments of the week

3. Losses: 1–3 areas of commitments you failed on

4. Fixes: What will you do next week to ensure it doesn't happen again?

5. Ahas: Greatest learning experiences throughout the week

6. Solicit needed feedback: To hold each other accountable

Peak Performance Weekly Questions

Month _____   Week _____

1. Most Important: Weekly focuses

2. Wins: 1–3 major accomplishments of the week

3. Losses: 1–3 areas of commitments you failed on

4. Fixes: What will you do next week to ensure it doesn't happen again?

5. Ahas: Greatest learning experiences throughout the week

6. Solicit needed feedback: To hold each other accountable

Peak Performance Weekly Questions

Month _____ Week _____

1. Most Important: Weekly focuses

2. Wins: 1–3 major accomplishments of the week

3. Losses: 1–3 areas of commitments you failed on

4. Fixes: What will you do next week to ensure it doesn't happen again?

5. Ahas: Greatest learning experiences throughout the week

6. Solicit needed feedback: To hold each other accountable

Peak Performance Weekly Questions

Month _____ Week _____

1. Most Important: Weekly focuses

2. Wins: 1–3 major accomplishments of the week

3. Losses: 1–3 areas of commitments you failed on

4. Fixes: What will you do next week to ensure it doesn't happen again?

5. Ahas: Greatest learning experiences throughout the week

6. Solicit needed feedback: To hold each other accountable

Peak Performance Weekly Questions

Month _____ Week _____

1. Most Important: Weekly focuses

2. Wins: 1–3 major accomplishments of the week

3. Losses: 1–3 areas of commitments you failed on

4. Fixes: What will you do next week to ensure it doesn't happen again?

5. Ahas: Greatest learning experiences throughout the week

6. Solicit needed feedback: To hold each other accountable

Peak Performance Weekly Questions

Month _____   Week _____

1. Most Important: Weekly focuses

2. Wins:1–3 major accomplishments of the week

3. Losses:1–3 areas of commitments you failed on

4. Fixes: What will you do next week to ensure it doesn't happen again?

5. Ahas: Greatest learning experiences throughout the week

6. Solicit needed feedback: To hold each other accountable

Peak Performance Weekly Questions

Month _____ Week _____

1. Most Important: Weekly focuses

2. Wins: 1–3 major accomplishments of the week

3. Losses: 1–3 areas of commitments you failed on

4. Fixes: What will you do next week to ensure it doesn't happen again?

5. Ahas: Greatest learning experiences throughout the week

6. Solicit needed feedback: To hold each other accountable

Peak Performance Weekly Questions

Month _____ Week _____

1. Most Important: Weekly focuses

2. Wins: 1–3 major accomplishments of the week

3. Losses: 1–3 areas of commitments you failed on

4. Fixes: What will you do next week to ensure it doesn't happen again?

5. Ahas: Greatest learning experiences throughout the week

6. Solicit needed feedback: To hold each other accountable

Peak Performance Weekly Questions

Month _____ Week _____

1. Most Important: Weekly focuses

2. Wins: 1–3 major accomplishments of the week

3. Losses: 1–3 areas of commitments you failed on

4. Fixes: What will you do next week to ensure it doesn't happen again?

5. Ahas: Greatest learning experiences throughout the week

6. Solicit needed feedback: To hold each other accountable

Peak Performance Weekly Questions

Month _____ Week _____

1. Most Important: Weekly focuses

2. Wins: 1–3 major accomplishments of the week

3. Losses: 1–3 areas of commitments you failed on

4. Fixes: What will you do next week to ensure it doesn't happen again?

5. Ahas: Greatest learning experiences throughout the week

6. Solicit needed feedback: To hold each other accountable

Peak Performance Weekly Questions

Month _____   Week _____

1. Most Important: Weekly focuses

2. Wins:1–3 major accomplishments of the week

3. Losses: 1–3 areas of commitments you failed on

4. Fixes: What will you do next week to ensure it doesn't happen again?

5. Ahas: Greatest learning experiences throughout the week

6. Solicit needed feedback: To hold each other accountable

Peak Performance Weekly Questions

Month _____ Week _____

1. Most Important: Weekly focuses

2. Wins: 1–3 major accomplishments of the week

3. Losses: 1–3 areas of commitments you failed on

4. Fixes: What will you do next week to ensure it doesn't happen again?

5. Ahas: Greatest learning experiences throughout the week

6. Solicit needed feedback: To hold each other accountable

Peak Performance Weekly Questions

Month _____   Week _____

1. Most Important: Weekly focuses

2. Wins: 1–3 major accomplishments of the week

3. Losses: 1–3 areas of commitments you failed on

4. Fixes: What will you do next week to ensure it doesn't happen again?

5. Ahas: Greatest learning experiences throughout the week

6. Solicit needed feedback: To hold each other accountable

WORKSHEET:
TURNING IDEAS INTO ACTION

Do this worksheet every month

I adapted this tool from the ***All Access EntreLeadership*** course I joined a few years ago (which, by the way, I highly recommend). This is a great tool to use for your business: it will help you stay focused on your priorities. I like to use this worksheet in our leadership team meetings.

MONTHLY

Turning Ideas Into Action

4 Insights

This excercise will help you prioritize the areas of your business on which you need to focus in the next quarter. Using the table below, list five things in your business that are *working*, five things that are *broken*, five things that are *confused* and five things that are *missing*.

MONTHLY

Working	Broken	Confused	Missing

Top 3 Priorities

Focusing only on the top priorities over the next 90 days will allow you to make significant progress—gaining traction on your overall goals. List them below:

1 _____

_____

2 _____

_____

3 _____

_____

Turning Ideas Into Action

4 Insights

This excercise will help you prioritize the areas of your business on which you need to focus in the next quarter. Using the table below, list five things in your business that are *working*, five things that are *broken*, five things that are *confused* and five things that are *missing*.

Working	Broken	Confused	Missing

MONTHLY

Top 3 Priorities

Focusing only on the top priorities over the next 90 days will allow you to make significant progress—gaining traction on your overall goals. List them below:

1 _____

_____

2 _____

_____

3 _____

_____

MONTHLY

Turning Ideas Into Action

4 Insights

This excercise will help you prioritize the areas of your business on which you need to focus in the next quarter. Using the table below, list five things in your business that are *working*, five things that are *broken*, five things that are *confused* and five things that are *missing*.

Working	Broken	Confused	Missing

Top 3 Priorities

Focusing only on the top priorities over the next 90 days will allow you to make significant progress—gaining traction on your overall goals. List them **below:**

1 _____

2 _____

3 _____

Turning Ideas Into Action

4 Insights

This excercise will help you prioritize the areas of your business on which you need to focus in the next quarter. Using the table below, list five things in your business that are *working*, five things that are *broken*, five things that are *confused* and five things that are *missing*.

Working	Broken	Confused	Missing

MONTHLY

Top 3 Priorities

Focusing only on the top priorities over the next 90 days will allow you to make significant progress—gaining traction on your overall goals. List them **below:**

1 _____

2 _____

3 _____

Turning Ideas Into Action

4 Insights

This excercise will help you prioritize the areas of your business on which you need to focus in the next quarter. Using the table below, list five things in your business that are *working*, five things that are *broken*, five things that are *confused* and five things that are *missing*.

Working	Broken	Confused	Missing

Top 3 Priorities

Focusing only on the top priorities over the next 90 days will allow you to make significant progress—gaining traction on your overall goals. List them **below:**

1 _____
_____

2 _____
_____

3 _____
_____

Turning Ideas Into Action

4 Insights

This excercise will help you prioritize the areas of your business on which you need to focus in the next quarter. Using the table below, list five things in your business that are *working*, five things that are *broken*, five things that are *confused* and five things that are *missing*.

Working	Broken	Confused	Missing

MONTHLY

Top 3 Priorities

Focusing only on the top priorities over the next 90 days will allow you to make significant progress—gaining traction on your overall goals. List them below:

1 _____

_____

2 _____

_____

3 _____

_____

Turning Ideas Into Action

4 Insights

This excercise will help you prioritize the areas of your business on which you need to focus in the next quarter. Using the table below, list five things in your business that are *working*, five things that are *broken*, five things that are *confused* and five things that are *missing*.

Working	Broken	Confused	Missing

Top 3 Priorities

Focusing only on the top priorities over the next 90 days will allow you to make significant progress—gaining traction on your overall goals. List them **below:**

1 _____

_____

2 _____

_____

3 _____

_____

Turning Ideas Into Action

4 Insights

This excercise will help you prioritize the areas of your business on which you need to focus in the next quarter. Using the table below, list five things in your business that are *working*, five things that are *broken*, five things that are *confused* and five things that are *missing*.

Working	Broken	Confused	Missing

MONTHLY

Top 3 Priorities

Focusing only on the top priorities over the next 90 days will allow you to make significant progress—gaining traction on your overall goals. List them **below:**

1 _____

_____

2 _____

_____

3 _____

_____

Turning Ideas Into Action

4 Insights

This excercise will help you prioritize the areas of your business on which you need to focus in the next quarter. Using the table below, list five things in your business that are *working*, five things that are *broken*, five things that are *confused* and five things that are *missing*.

MONTHLY

Working	Broken	Confused	Missing

Top 3 Priorities

Focusing only on the top priorities over the next 90 days will allow you to make significant progress—gaining traction on your overall goals. List them below:

1 _____
_____

2 _____
_____

3 _____
_____

Turning Ideas Into Action

4 Insights

This excercise will help you prioritize the areas of your business on which you need to focus in the next quarter. Using the table below, list five things in your business that are *working*, five things that are *broken*, five things that are *confused* and five things that are *missing*.

Working	Broken	Confused	Missing

MONTHLY

Top 3 Priorities

Focusing only on the top priorities over the next 90 days will allow you to make significant progress—gaining traction on your overall goals. List them **below:**

1 _____

_____

2 _____

_____

3 _____

_____

Turning Ideas Into Action

4 Insights

This excercise will help you prioritize the areas of your business on which you need to focus in the next quarter. Using the table below, list five things in your business that are *working*, five things that are *broken*, five things that are *confused* and five things that are *missing*.

Working	Broken	Confused	Missing

Top 3 Priorities

Focusing only on the top priorities over the next 90 days will allow you to make significant progress—gaining traction on your overall goals. List them **below:**

1 _____

_____

2 _____

_____

3 _____

_____

Turning Ideas Into Action

4 Insights

This excercise will help you prioritize the areas of your business on which you need to focus in the next quarter. Using the table below, list five things in your business that are *working*, five things that are *broken*, five things that are *confused* and five things that are *missing*.

Working	Broken	Confused	Missing

MONTHLY

Top 3 Priorities

Focusing only on the top priorities over the next 90 days will allow you to make significant progress—gaining traction on your overall goals. List them **below:**

1 _____

_____

2 _____

_____

3 _____

_____

WORKSHEET:
PRIORITY MANAGEMENT

Do this worksheet every month

It honestly isn't about TIME management, it's about PRIORITY management. You can manage all the time you want doing the WRONG things, but this worksheet helps you prioritize what you NEED to accomplish, not just what would be NICE to accomplish. I fill out this form every single month.

Step 1: Use the first column to list your priorities for the month (up to 5). Refer to the 21 Habits to Become a Great Leader worksheet, your Balance Wheel, and your Personal Development Plan.

Step 2: In the middle column, list your signs of success. Describe in detail how success would look and feel.

Step 3: Use the last column to list your creative masters: the people you can empower, enlist, or hire to help you accomplish your priorities.

Month _____

Priority	Signs of Success	Creative Masters
1		
2		
3		
4		
5		

Month _____

Priority	Signs of Success	Creative Masters
1		
2		
3		
4		
5		

MONTHLY

Month _____

MONTHLY

Priority	Signs of Success	Creative Masters
1		
2		
3		
4		
5		

Month _____

Priority	Signs of Success	Creative Masters
1		
2		
3		
4		
5		

MONTHLY

Month _____

Priority	Signs of Success	Creative Masters
1		
2		
3		
4		
5		

MONTHLY

Month _____

Priority	Signs of Success	Creative Masters
1		
2		
3		
4		
5		

Month _____

MONTHLY

Priority	Signs of Success	Creative Masters
1		
2		
3		
4		
5		

Month _____

Priority	Signs of Success	Creative Masters
1		
2		
3		
4		
5		

MONTHLY

Month _____

MONTHLY

Priority		Signs of Success	Creative Masters
	1		
	2		
	3		
	4		
	5		

Month _____

Priority	Signs of Success	Creative Masters
1		
2		
3		
4		
5		

MONTHLY

Month _____

Priority	Signs of Success	Creative Masters
1		
2		
3		
4		
5		

MONTHLY

Month _____

Priority	Signs of Success	Creative Masters
1		
2		
3		
4		
5		

MONTHLY

WORKSHEET:
Balance Wheel

Do this worksheet every quarter

This is my all-time favorite tool. I started implementing it in my life in 2002, and I've created dozens of different balance wheels since then. I teach this in my leadership workshops—there's barely a class that goes by when I don't at least hit on this topic. WHY? Because the highest form of leadership is leading yourself. You can't give what you don't have.

I have frequently witnessed not only myself but also my team members who struggle personally and professionally when these areas aren't fulfilled. The trick is to find your top two non-negotiables and focus on them at all times. For instance, I know that when my spiritual and physical areas are left unfulfilled and empty, I'm a wreck! My self-esteem suffers, my mind suffers, my family suffers, my team suffers!

Use the first page of the Balance Wheel worksheet to take inventory of what you're currently doing well, where you need improvement, and your goals for each area. On the second page, rate your current status in each area using a scale of 0 to 10, with 10 being the highest. Color in the section from the 0 mark up to the mark you gave yourself. What does your wheel look like?

Once you see your balance wheel results, you can make action plans for any areas you want to improve. Once you set up your action plans, commit to being intentional about focusing on each area. My action plans go right into my planner—I write them down!

"A healthy self-worth creates a wealthy net worth."

Category	What I'm Doing Well	Where I Need Improvement	My Goals
Attitude			
Career			
Finance			
Personal Growth			
Health			
Family			
Relationships			
Social Life			

QUARTERLY

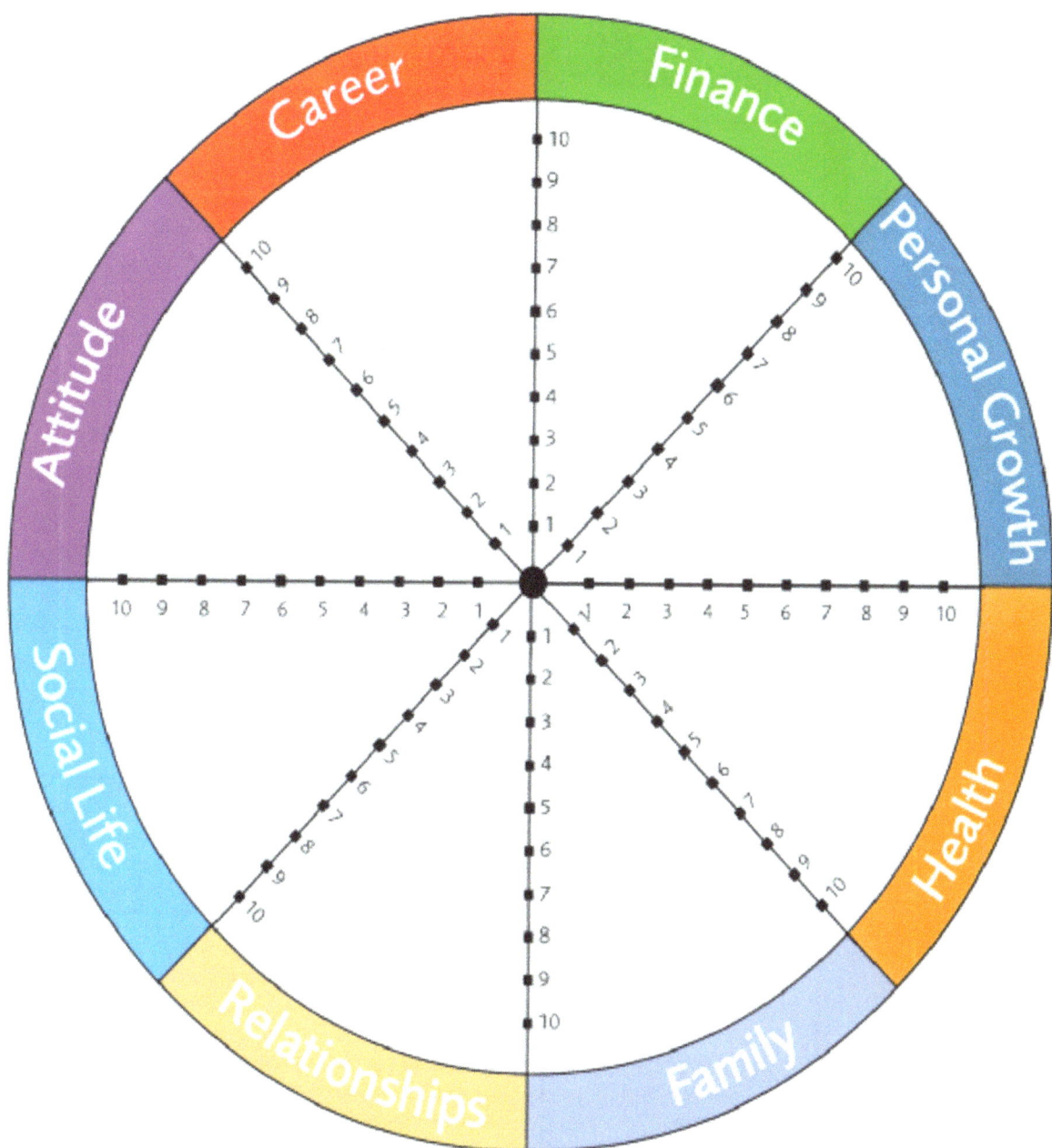

381

Category	What I'm Doing Well	Where I Need Improvement	My Goals
Attitude			
Career			
Finance			
Personal Growth			
Health			
Family			
Relationships			
Social Life			

QUARTERLY

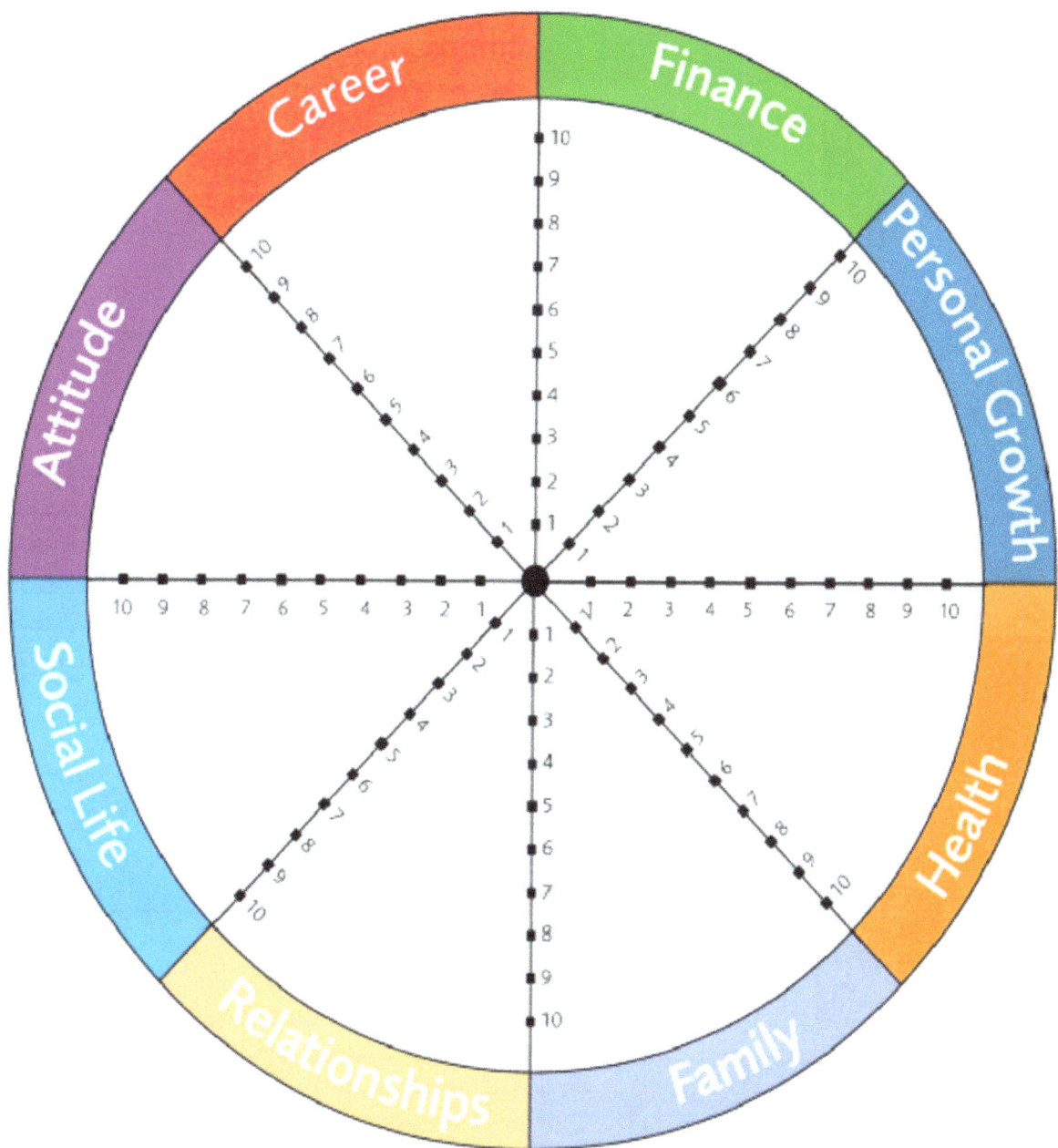

QUARTERLY

Category	What I'm Doing Well	Where I Need Improvement	My Goals
Attitude			
Career			
Finance			
Personal Growth			
Health			
Family			
Relationships			
Social Life			

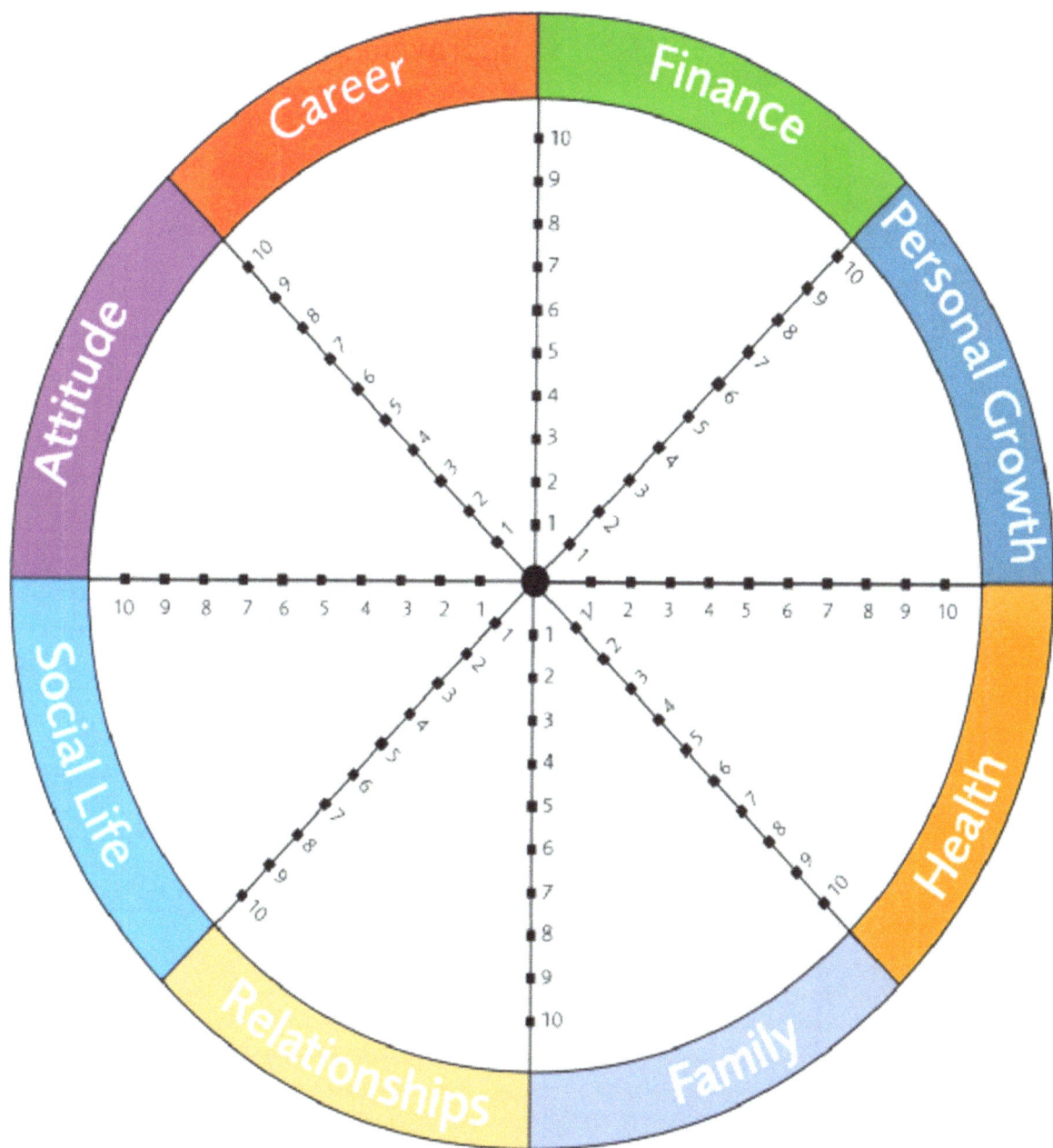

385

BALANCE WHEEL WORKSHEET

Category	What I'm Doing Well	Where I Need Improvement	My Goals
Attitude			
Career			
Finance			
Personal Growth			
Health			
Family			
Relationships			
Social Life			

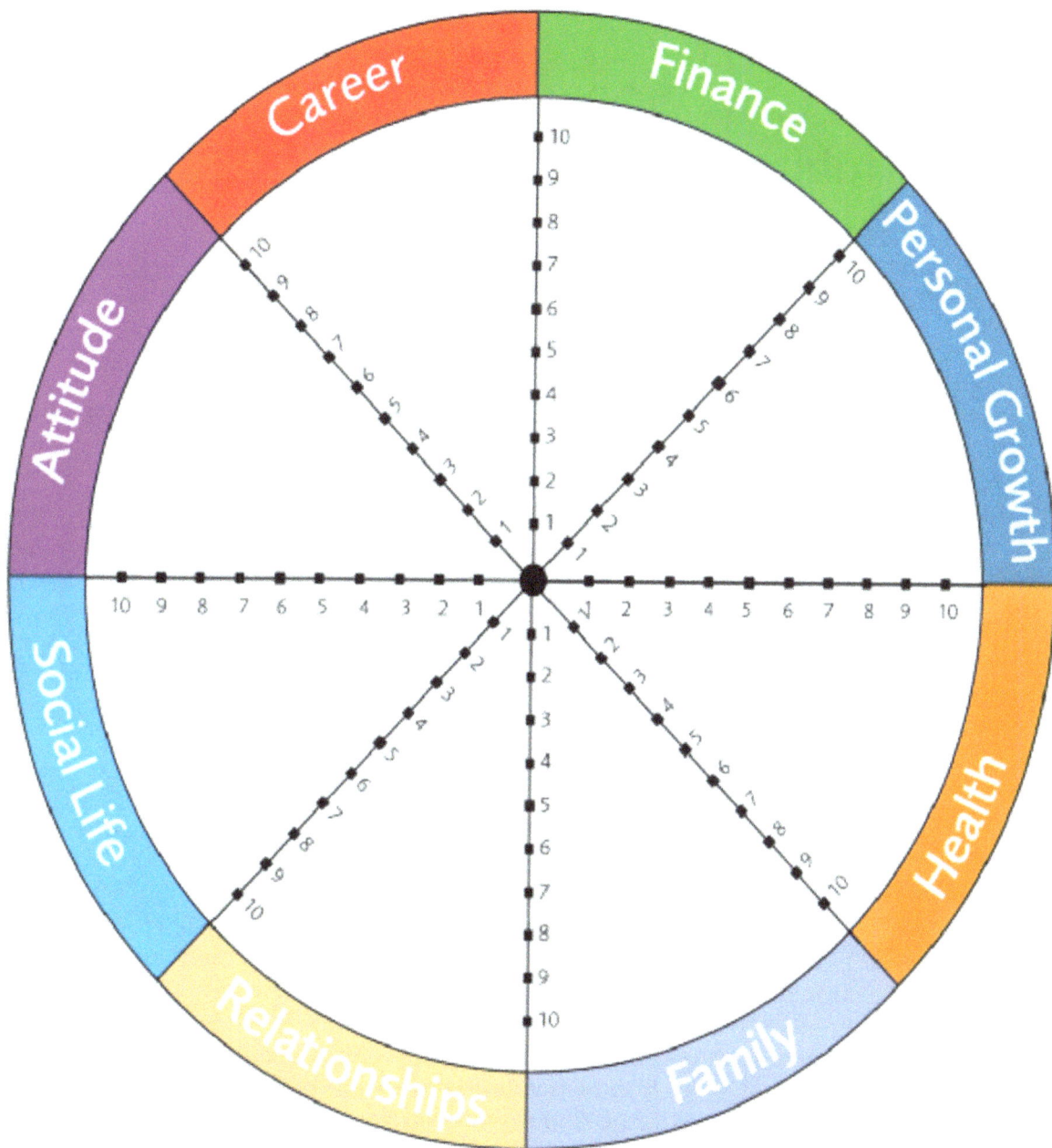

387

WORSHEET:
21 Habits to Become a Great Leader

Do this worksheet every year

Being a planner first and foremost requires you to be a leader. In fact, I wrote my second book, *BE A LEADER*, to get people excited about journaling and growing their leadership ... but the journey starts with growing YOU. You can't influence others if you first haven't been influenced (or, as I like to say, transformed). Transformed people transform people!

I teach leadership workshops all over the country, and when I ask people what the highest form of leadership is, they stare at me blankly—just like I did with my leadership coach, John C. Maxwell in 2013, when he asked me that question. Little did I know that the highest form of leadership is leading ourselves. When I ask the second question—How do you lead yourself?—I get more blank stares. So I've included a fun little worksheet, *The 21 Habits to Become a Great Leader*, to get you started.

Remember, growing yourself isn't much easier than going to the gym, so make it FUN!

The first rule for this worksheet is to use FUN COLORED MARKERS (I love Mr. Scented), and go to a quiet area, play some soft meditational music, and light a candle.

Now peruse the 21 Habits to Become a Great Leader. Check all the boxes that are already consistent habits in your life and highlight the ones you have not made into habits yet. Use a red marker to put stars on the top three boxes that you'd love to make a habit this year.

21 Habits to Become a Great Leader

Wake up and go to bed **EARLY**

Make your bed **EVERY MORNING**

Drink a **BIG GLASS OF WATER** as soon as you wake up

Work out until you **SWEAT**

Morning + evening **MEDITATION**

Put on **CLOTHES** that make you **FEEL GOOD,** even if you're at home today

Write out **YOUR GOALS** to remind yourself what you're working for

MAKE A PLAN for your day

Spend an hour on your **ONE THING**

Have a **GREEN SMOOTHIE**

Do one thing you've been **PUTTING OFF**

1 hour of **LEARNING:** books, podcasts, online courses

POST a thought online—a short blog post, picture, or new idea

Send someone you know a **NICE MESSAGE**

Come up with **5 NEW IDEAS**

Give a **SMILE** or **COMPLIMENT** to a stranger

DECLUTTER 1 item every day

MAKE A LIST for tomorrow to clear your mind before you sleep

GRATITUDE: Think of 3 things you appreciate in your life

REVIEW the Day: What **WORKED?** What **Didn't?**

Go outside for a **WALK**

YEARLY

389

WORSHEET:
YEAR IN REVIEW WORKSHEET

Do this worksheet at the end of the year

I recommend that you start filling this out at the beginning of December, so you can take your time. Along with this annual review, I also plan my WORD FOR THE YEAR.

I don't set New Year's resolutions but I do choose ONE WORD for the year. I adopted this idea from Jon Gordon's book, *One Word that Will Change Your Life*, and it has been a habit of mine since 2012.

For example, my word this year is PRESENT, inspired by Psalm 16:11: "In your presence is fullness of joy."

What's your one word this year?

_____

Year in Review

Ten greatest happenings from last year:

1._____   6._____

2._____   7._____

3._____   8._____

4._____   9._____

5._____   10._____

I am most proud of these three accomplishments from last year:

1._____

2._____

3._____

Three greatest lessons I've learned from last year:

1._____

2._____

3._____

Three personal improvements I've made in the past year:

1._____

2._____

3._____

If I could go back and do it again, I would do these three things differently last year:

1._____

2._____

3._____

The greatest influences (products, people viewpoints, other) on me in the last year:

_____

_____

Smartest decision I made last year:

_____

Most caring service I performed last year:

_____

Biggest risk I took last year:

_____

Most important relationship improved last year:

_____

One word that best sums up and describes last year's experience:

_____

Three things I need to do less in the next year:

1._____
2._____
3._____

Three things I need to do more in the next year:

1._____
2._____
3._____

Three things I need to stop doing altogether in the next year:

1._____
2._____
3._____

YEARLY

Excerpted from Living Your Best Year Ever by Darren Hardy

WORKSHEET:
PERSONAL DEVELOPMENT PLAN

Do this worksheet every year

As I mentioned earlier, when I ask people what the highest form of leadership is, I get a lot of blank stares. The highest form of leadership is leading ourselves. We don't have to fix and change our kids, our spouse, our parents, our boss, our staff, or anyone else. All we have to do is fix and change ourselves and then stand back and watch everyone around us grow! *YES, it really is that easy!*

When I ask the obvious follow-up question—"What is your personal growth plan this year?"—I get even more blank stares, so I developed a worksheet for designing my growth plan year after year. You'll find the worksheet on the next page ... but first take a look at my sample growth plan for this year. Keep in mind that mine changes year after year, too.

Everything in this **BE A PLANNER** are the tools I use to constantly develop my growth plan. Here is a sample of what I do daily/weekly to grow myself.

PROFESSIONAL:

QUARTERLY MASTERMINDS with BUSINESS LEADERS

BOOKS PLANNED TO UTILIZE THIS YEAR:

- *Daring Greatly* by Brené Brown
- *The 5 Languages of Appreciation in the Workplace*
- *The Power of WHY*
- *Emotional Intelligence 2.0*
- *Be Nice (Or Else!)* by Winn Claybaugh
- *Switch On Your Brain*
- *Profit First*
- *Developing the Leader Within You 2.0*
- *The Ideal Team Player*
- *The Leadership Handbook*
- *The Maxwell Leadership Bible*
- *The 360 Degree Leader*

...continued on next page

Tina's Personal Development Plan continued...

John Maxwell team website:

- Choose a message from the website to study for at least 1 hour a day
- EntreLeadership All Access coaching, monthly mastermind, and 1 hour a week e-coaching

Weekly podcasts *(listen at least 1 hour a day)*:

- Entreleadership
- Patrice Washington
- Joyce Meyer

PHYSICAL:

- **Daily post in T's BEACH BODY** – Inspirational quotes and messages to hold myself and team accountable (yes, you can join this FREE private Facebook page anytime - meant to inspire and help hold you accountable to your fitness goals)

SPIRITUAL/EMOTIONAL HEALTH:

- Daily Bible study utilizing the book devotional: *My Time With God* by Joyce Meyer
- Shawn Bolz webinars
- Bill Johnson's books and podcasts
- Marriage Bible study utilizing John Maxwell's *Leadership Bible*
- Tim Storey's weekly messages

INTELLECTUAL:

Books and podcasts by Dr. Caroline Leaf:
- *Switch On Your Brain*
- *Quarterly 21-Day Brain Detox*

Personal Development Plan

What is my goal?

Why do I want to do it?

When will I achieve it?

How will I do it exactly?

What will count as a success?

What do I need to remember?

What am I good at?

What would I like to be better at?

What would I like to know more about?

What kind of skills would I like to have?

"Growth is the only guarantee that tomorrow will be better."
John C. Maxwell

WORSHEET:
DREAM BOARD

Create this dream board every year

Every year I coach my team and my clients to make a dream board—or even better, a dream wall! Don't limit the space you have to dream. I normally use a pasteboard every year, then take a picture of it and keep it in my planner.

You can take a picture of yours and glue it on the following page so you always have it with you:

1. During the last three months of the year, collect pictures, words, and quotes from magazines, Pinterest, etc., on the goals you want to reach.

2. During the last few weeks of the year, paste or staple your quotes, pictures, and words onto your pasteboard or wall.

3. Sign up for one of my masterminds and get a personal "reading" of your dream board. ☺

PUT YOUR DREAM BOARD HERE:

BE
BE A PLANNER

I hope this planner has inspired you to live your best year ever!

Please let me know your thoughts on this planner
and how I can make it even better for next year!

GOD BLESS,
TINA BLACK

For additional copies of any of the worksheets
you can go to my website *www.TinaBlack.net*
and use the access code: *BE*